How Fast,

Inexpensive,

Restrained, and

Elegant Methods

Ignite Innovation

DAN WARD

HARPER
BUSINESS

An Imprint of HarperCollins*Publishers*
www.harpercollins.com

The views expressed in this book are solely those of the author and do not reflect the official policy or position of the US Air Force or Department of Defense.

HarperCollins books may be purchased for educational, business, or sales promotional use. For information, please e-mail the Special Markets Department at SPsales@harpercollins.com.

The line drawing in figure 7.4 (Struve and Telescheff's Flying Machine) is by Octave Chanute, from his book *Progress in Flying Machines*, which is in the public domain. All other figures are by the author.

FIRST EDITION

Designed by Adam B. Bohannon

Library of Congress Cataloging-in-Publication Data has been applied for.

ISBN: 978-0-06-230190-1

14 15 16 17 18   OV/RRD   10 9 8 7 6 5 4 3 2 1

To Kim, Bethany, and Jenna

CONTENTS

In 2003, I coined the acronym FIST (Fast, Inexpensive, Simple, Tiny) to describe the US military's approach to high-speed, low-cost innovation. This method uses constraints to foster creativity and, through a thoughtful application of speed, thrift, simplicity, and restraint, has a track record of producing best-in-class and first-in-class technologies. Of course the Pentagon doesn't always build new equipment this way, but FIST was my attempt to document how the military technology community functions when it is at its best.

Over the next decade, I refined the idea in a series of journal articles, conference presentations, and superhero comics, incorporating lessons from government entities like NASA and companies like Apple. My buddies and I implemented this approach on half a dozen projects, and along the way we built a wider network of "unindicted co-conspirators" who used FIST methods and techniques to build everything from spacecraft to software. FIST was the central topic of my master's degree thesis at the Air Force Institute of Technology and became a defining feature of my military career.

As my time in uniform came to an end, it seemed a reboot was in order. After much thought and discussion, a new acronym emerged: FIRE (Fast, Inexpensive, Restrained, Elegant). While FIST aimed to reduce the time, cost, and complexity associated with developing new *military* gear, FIRE extends these methods to applications beyond the battlefield. The idea was to take the concept from the profession of arms and bring it to the marketplace, essentially turning the sword into a plowshare. If only all weapons could undergo a similar transformation.

Many of the stories that follow are about military equipment or NASA missions, of course, because that's the world I come from. The principles and techniques, however, are relevant in a much wider range of situations and can produce technology for all sorts of uses. I hope you enjoy the stories and have fun using the methods. I hope it helps you change the world for the better.

Aim high,
Dan Ward

CHAPTER 1

The FIRE Method

In December 2010 at a tiny research facility in freezing-cold Rome, New York, US Air Force scientists cut the ribbon on a supercomputer named the Condor Cluster. Operating at 500 TFLOPS—trillion floating-point operations per second—it was the fastest supercomputer in the entire Department of Defense and the thirty-third fastest in the world. Contributing to its awesomeness was the price tag—the Air Force only paid 10 percent of what it would cost for a comparable supercomputer. On top of that, the Condor Cluster uses a mere 10 percent of the electricity typically required by similar machines, which means it's got a smaller carbon footprint and is less expensive to operate. Not a bad day's work.

One other interesting fact about the Condor Cluster: it was built out of 1,760 Sony PlayStations. True story.

In other parts of the Department of Defense, results were decidedly less awesome. Just three months earlier, in September 2010, the Supreme Court agreed to hear arguments related to the US Navy's A-12 Avenger airplane, known to some as the Flying Dorito because of its triangular shape. Begun in 1983 and envisioned as an all-weather, carrier-based stealth bomber/attack jet, the Avenger program was terminated in 1991, at which point the Navy had spent $2 billion but received nothing for its money beyond a really exciting case study in failure for students at the Defense Acquisition University.

After almost twenty years of litigation, the nation's highest court was finally going to consider whether the government's decision to cancel this bloated project was justified. Resolution was apparently not to be, and in May 2011 the court returned the case to the lower appeals court instead of deciding, so the saga continued.

We could spend all day looking at similar examples from all the military services, highlighting the ups and downs of defense technology. The Army, Navy, Marine Corps, and Air Force all have their own stories of critical new gear being delivered in a matter of weeks, right alongside stories where billions and decades are spent to deliver exactly nothing. Of course, these highs and lows are not limited to the military. NASA has some of the best failure and success stories around, and the pages that follow present several of each. For that matter, the federal government does not have a monopoly here, and as the book progresses we'll look at stories from the private world as well—portable music players, household appliances, and science toys, to name a few. But before we consider any particular stories, let's look at the disparities among them in general terms.

Why do some programs deliver their product under budget, while others see their costs expand by orders of magnitude? Why do some deliver ahead of schedule, while others experience endless delay after endless delay? And, most critically, which products work better—the quick and thrifty, or the slow and expensive? Which situation leads to superior equipment?

After a few years of conducting informal research into these questions, I spent eighteen months at the Air Force Institute of Technology looking at them more rigorously. The pattern that emerged is this: the most successful project leaders from government and industry alike tend to deliver top-shelf stuff with a skeleton crew, a shoestring budget, and a cannonball schedule. In interviews I read and those I personally conducted, project leaders continually echoed one theme: "We had no time and no money. We were just lucky to have a small team of really creative, dedicated people and we got it done."

In contrast, project leaders who are cursed with large budgets, large teams, and long schedules generally have a difficult time delivering even a fraction of the promised capability, an outcome often blamed on an excessively cumbersome process. Interestingly, when faced with cancellation due to severe cost overruns and delays, these leaders typically respond, "If I had a little more time and money, I could fix this."

Yes, those who had the largest budgets were most likely to ask for more money and least likely to deliver an actual working product. Those with the smallest budgets were most likely to have cash left over after delivering ten pounds of awesome on a five-pound purse. For reasons we'll examine shortly, the faster, cheaper stuff also tends to perform better in actual use than the slower, more expensive stuff.

The idea that spending less time and money leads to better outcomes sounds a bit like claiming that moderate amounts of red wine and dark chocolate are good for you. Surely this is too good to be true. And yet, as with the aforementioned health benefits, the data is compelling. In the pages that follow, we'll take a closer look at exactly when, how, and why the FIRE approach leads to superior equipment and products. Be forewarned: just because FIRE is possible does not mean it is necessarily easy to implement, but I'm sure you didn't come here looking for easy answers.

We haven't said much about complexity yet, so let's remedy that right now. Successful project leaders tend to place a premium on simplicity in their organizations, processes, documentation, and technologies. They tend to view simplicity as a desirable attribute and pursue opportunities to simplify when they are able. Later in the book we'll see some tools that will help us do precisely that.

FIRE codifies the practices, principles, and tools used by some of the best technology developers in the world— people who sent spacecraft on intercept courses with asteroids or who built fighter planes that dominated the skies of World War II. FIRE also describes the way clever toy designers teach science lessons that are actually fun. In the stories that follow, we'll see that project leaders who embrace speed, thrift, simplicity, and restraint tend to deliver affordable equipment that is available when it's needed and effective when it's used. You'll learn how to do that too.

One final note: while improving one's process might be a fun way to spend a sunny July afternoon, FIRE is emphatically not a process improvement initiative. Given the modern popularity of process improvement methodologies, that last sentiment bears repeating: FIRE is not about process improvement.

The primary objective is to improve our *objectives* and

outcomes rather than our *processes*. There is a tremendous difference between them. Clever project leaders should certainly make an effort to streamline, simplify, and accelerate their processes, but the bulk of their attention is rightfully spent on the product itself and on taking care of the people who make it.

The reason for this is simple. Process-centric improvement efforts have a maddening tendency to be process-centric, despite official protests to the contrary. This myopic orientation frequently overshadows both the team members and the product itself, and instead focuses on delivering a set of lovely, full-color, hypothetical process flow diagrams that signify nothing.

In contrast, FIRE is all about helping *people* make good *decisions* as we design and create new things. Accordingly, this book presents a set of practical heuristics—rules of thumb designed to help actual people make good decisions. These little guidelines don't dictate behavior; nor do they represent a step-by-step formula. Good luck trying to build a process flow diagram out of them. Instead, the heuristic approach echoes Visa CEO Dee Hock's explanation of how he succeeded in founding the Visa credit card association: "We have no precise plan, only a clear sense of direction."

Before we get to the guidelines themselves, we need to take a closer look at the four components of FIRE, to see how they combine to foster that "clear sense of direction."

F Is for Fast

The F in FIRE stands for *fast*, which says it's important and good to have a short schedule. It's about defining a project objective that can be satisfied on a short timeline, not one we know full well will require twenty years to accomplish.

Now, the precise definition of "short timeline" will naturally vary from context to context. Some applications might deliver new capabilities every day and be considered hopelessly slow if they clock in on a monthly schedule, while for others, delivering in a year would represent a world-class commitment to speed. For military technology, a 2008 report from the Government Accountability Office says "system development should be limited to about five years," and anything longer than that probably counts as "slow." The point is, there is some amount of time that represents rapid delivery, so aim for that.

Being fast means we don't try to solve problems by adding days to the schedule. As the book progresses, we'll look at some strategies for speed to help us accelerate our development timelines and to solve problems using more thoughtful techniques than simply asking for more time. The key is to treat the schedule as a constraint to be lived with, not as a starting point to be extended later.

Although process improvement is not a central aspect of FIRE, it does have something to say about process. Specifically, FIRE proposes designing our organizations and processes with speed in mind and remaining on the lookout for opportunities to remove speed bumps from the process. This is where process improvement techniques can come in handy. The difference is that FIRE treats these techniques as tools rather than goals, as mechanisms to help achieve a larger objective rather than an objective to be pursued for its own sake—as so often happens in process-centric approaches.

As a general rule, speed is good. Slow kills. Speed fosters stability within a program and reduces our exposure to the forces of change. Speed enhances accountability and learning for the team members. Speed increases the likelihood that the product will be well aligned with both the market's interest and the available technologies.

But here is the twist: we must not be content with the superficial appearance of speed, where we appear to be moving quickly but are in fact spinning our wheels or running in the wrong direction. Nor should we pursue speed at the expense of doing good work. This means no cutting corners, no skipping essential steps in the development process. The project is only fast if we do *quality* work on a short timeline.

For example, most of the time we still need to design, document, and test the thing we are building. Rather than skipping those activities entirely or accomplishing them halfheartedly, FIRE offers ways to perform each essential step with speed in mind. So a performance test may only take a minute instead of a year, and it may be performed simultaneously with other activities, but failing to do any tests at all is not what we have in mind when we talk about being fast.

Remember the lesson from the famous race in Aesop's fable: the tortoise was faster than the hare because he got to the finish line first. So by all means, be fast. But don't be hasty.

There is also a big difference between being fast and being frantic. Fast is about speed with discipline, focused speed that efficiently moves us from where we are toward where we need to go. Frantic activity, in contrast, spins in circles and creates the appearance of rapidity without actually producing much in the way of forward momentum. Running around like a chicken with its hair on fire is the antithesis of productive action, no matter how exciting it might feel.

I Is for Inexpensive

The I in FIRE—for *inexpensive*—says it's important to have a small budget. That may be an unpopular position in an environment in which budgets equal prestige, but in my experience I've found that the ability to deliver meaningful capabilities on a shoestring is actually a widely respected skill, even in the cash-rich defense business. Ask yourself: Would you rather be known as the person who manages a $50 billion project that is late or over budget, or the guy who makes great things happen without busting the bank? Which one do you think makes a better impact? Who sleeps better at night—the guy in charge of building the second Death Star, which is so far behind schedule it requires a Sith Lord to straighten things out, or Q, the head of James Bond's quartermaster division, who always has a freshly tweaked vehicle ready for Her Majesty's secret agent to take on his next mission?

Being inexpensive is about designing our organizations and processes with thrift in mind and solving problems with intellectual capital instead of financial capital. It's about setting program goals that can be satisfied on lean budgets and finding thrifty ways to perform even the expensive-sounding functions. The key is to treat the budget as a constraint, not a starting point to be expanded later. It's a ceiling, not a floor.

But just as fast does not mean hasty, inexpensive is not the same as cheap. You see, a low-cost solution that doesn't work is actually a pretty expensive solution. Inexpensive does not mean simply picking the low bidder or settling for an inadequate component. What we're trying to do is maximize bang for the buck, get the most rumble for our rubles, the most sound for our pound.

R Is for Restrained

The third piece of FIRE stands for *restrained*. This is the common thread that runs through the whole FIRE concept. It is a preference for self-control, for tight budgets and small teams, for short schedules, short meetings, and short documents.

Yes, there's a point at which an organization isn't large enough to do the work, and a point at which a document or briefing doesn't convey all the necessary information. As a general rule, we could get a lot closer to that boundary than we typically do. To demonstrate this, that's all I'm going to say about restraint.

E Is for Elegant

The E in FIRE stands for *elegant*, in the sense of "pleasingly ingenious and simple." Simplicity is an ironically complex topic and will be covered in future chapters, so for now let's start by pointing out that it is important and good to have a low level of complexity. This sentiment may seem obvious, but given so many people's love affair with complexity, I think it is worth saying out loud.

Embracing elegant simplicity means designing our organizations and processes with simplicity in mind. It's about stating our goals clearly and incorporating mature, proven technologies into our designs. True sophistication, true design maturity, and true process maturity are shown through deep simplicity, not through brain-meltingly complex diagrams and structures. In other words, complexity is nothing to brag about.

A certain degree of complexity is inevitable in any situation. While we may not be able to avoid complexity entirely, we can certainly take steps to minimize it. But merely simplifying our design without making it better is a superficial application of simplicity. For simplicity to be elegant and virtuous, it needs to improve the project's quality, performance, or usability. We'll look at several strategies for doing exactly that.

The FIRE Principles

Soldiers, spies, and other operatives who regularly face unpredictable scenarios must rely on tradecraft and ingenuity rather than rigidly defined procedures to accomplish their missions. Mastering tradecraft involves learning a set of general protocols to guide behavior and decision making in uncertain situations, then learning when and how to apply each one. Engineers, architects, and other skilled professionals have a similar approach, relying on broad heuristics and rules of thumb to solve specific problems as they emerge. Accordingly, FIRE is a heuristic-based approach.

Unlike a rule-based approach, FIRE presupposes that wisdom resides in the hearer and doer rather than in the rule itself. That is, a rule offers firm external instruction on what should or should not be done. A rule is itself the source of rightness, while the person reading or hearing the rule is the recipient. A rule-based approach focuses on compliance with predefined standards.

In contrast, a flexible guideline walks alongside us, like a companion. Where rules go before us and say, "Proceed thus, without deviation," heuristics and rules of thumb suggest rather than dictate, offering illumination rather than demanding imitation. In doing so they aim to draw wisdom out from the recipient, not stuff wisdom in. This more flexible approach acknowledges that the person doing the work is ultimately the source of goodness and is thus free to focus on outcomes rather than compliance. The outcome orientation is a critically important distinction and a significant strength compared to a strict rule-based approach.

Speaking of strength, a good rule of thumb conveys a depth of experience that goes beyond what can be captured in words on a page. This is both its great strength and its main weakness. Any attempt to define and explain a heuristic in writing will be partial at best. Text lacks the experiential context, hand gestures, and immediacy that accompany a teaching moment where one person says to another, "In this situation, I find it helps to do this," or "Here is how we generally approach this type of problem." That is why, even in this digital age, these informal principles are often passed along verbally, in person, rather than in writing. This reflects both the nature of heuristics and the nature of the work in question. Oral tradition helps ensure that the richness and wisdom of the rules are conveyed in a way that mere words on paper cannot easily express.

This does not place heuristics off-limits for writers. It just means any list of them will necessarily be entirely incomplete, ponderously long, or both. There are simply too many situations and too many guidelines to capture them in anything close to a comprehensive list.

Therefore, the following summary of principles is offered as a representative sample rather than a comprehensive listing. The explanations accompanying each one are mere introductions to the practice rather than a rigorous analysis of the theory. The objective is to indicate the *type* of thinking inherent in the FIRE approach, not to offer a definitive rule set. Please consider this a jumping-off point for your own reflection, discussion, and experimentation.

And as you read, keep in mind the words of John Keats: "Axioms in philosophy are not axioms until they are proved upon our pulses; we read fine things but never feel them to the full until we have gone the same steps as the author." The poet is right—if you want to really understand this stuff, it helps to actually do it.

YOU CANNOT DESIGN ANYTHING
WITHOUT REVEALING YOUR VALUES

Project management is fundamentally a decision-making discipline. It involves making decisions about topics ranging from process and organization to technical architectures and choices of materials. The decisions we make shape the project's outcomes, but the decisions themselves—particularly design decisions—are shaped by the preferences, priorities, and values of the decision maker. As my friend Dr. Joel Sercel puts it, you cannot design anything without revealing your values.

When we value complexity and consider it a sign of sophistication, we will naturally design complex things—processes, organizations, and software—because we see complexity as a sign of goodness. Similarly, if we equate budget size with prestige, we will hold a large budget in higher esteem than a small budget . . . and will pursue opportunities to increase rather than decrease the cost of our project. So when you see a complex, expensive design that took decades to complete, there's a pretty good chance the people behind that project held a low opinion of being fast, inexpensive, restrained, and elegant.

FIRE proposes a value set based on speed, thrift, simplicity, and self-control. It posits that these four attributes are productive values and, when used to shape our decision making, lead to desirable outcomes; thus, much of this book presents stories and data that support that proposition. But whether our decisions are shaped by the FIRE values or something else, it is wise to be aware of what we value and, as much as possible, to select values that are consistent with our objectives.

YOU CAN'T CHANGE JUST ONE THING

Let's call this Systems Engineering Rule 1. Everything is connected to something, so in all but the simplest situations, changes to one aspect will have implications for other parts of the system. In engineering terms, that means changing a vehicle's weight will affect its speed and handling. Programmatically, it means changes to the budget will likely affect the schedule. We may not intend to change more than one thing at a time, but it is virtually impossible for a change to be truly isolated. The idea is to be aware of the second-order effects of our changes and to not get caught by surprise when changes to A drive changes to B, C, and D.

In terms of implementing FIRE, this means we can't simply shorten the schedule but leave everything else the same and expect to get a good result. To get the full effect, we have to change more than one thing. Speed without thrift and simplicity is going to lead to a spectacular crash, so along with accelerating the schedule we'll also have to restrict the budget and reduce complexity.

This is not just about the product's design. We also have to change the way we interpret and implement our processes, the way we produce and review documents, maybe even the way the organization itself is structured (see earlier note about small teams). FIRE aims to provide a comprehensive framework for making changes across the spectrum of decision making rather than offering a tool to change just one or two aspects of the work.

CONSTRAINTS FOSTER CREATIVITY

When we do not have enough time, money, or manpower to pursue typical solutions, we are forced by circumstances to consider alternatives. This is a good thing. Constraints—temporal, financial, physical, or otherwise—take the obvious approach off the table and lead us toward the non-obvious. Frugality thus serves as a forcing function to stimulate imaginative thinking. The resulting excursion is often not only more creative, which can be virtuous in its own right, but also better and more focused. Perhaps this is why researchers at the Standish Group suggest that a particular class of information technology development programs should have "no more than four people, four months and $500,000." The specific numbers vary from context to context, but the data suggest that tight limits are paradoxically freeing.

If you have to tell your story in a six-word memoir or pitch your product in a three-minute elevator speech, you will find it quite possible, and the exercise will be wonderfully clarifying. The same goes for building your system on a $150 budget or writing code in a twenty-four-hour sprint.

The result of this minimalist approach, if done well, is a distilled essence of what really matters. Establishing strict constraints therefore can help prevent overengineered solutions, bloated software, and incoherent PowerPoint decks.

FOCUS FOSTERS SPEED

If your priorities are clear and your activities are oriented toward an overarching objective, you'll find that things move along with a minimal expenditure of time. Keeping the objective in sharp focus strips away distractions that slow us down. So one of the key FIRE disciplines is to establish and maintain a small list of Most Important Things. This list should not have more than three things on it. Any more than three, and we'll find ourselves bogged down, slowed down, and perpetually late to the party.

SPEED VALIDATES THE NEED

If we don't plan to acquire a new product for another decade, there's a good chance we don't really *need* it. That is, if we don't need it now, we can't really say for sure whether we'll need it ten years from now. It is much more accurate to say we have current *needs* and future *wants*.

A short-term due date indicates a greater degree of legitimacy than a long-term due date. When we need something right away, it's generally because we have a clear understanding of some capability gap. This does not mean there is no such thing as a long-term interest or that we should never undertake a lengthy project—bear in mind that this is a heuristic, not a rule. It simply suggests our ability to understand and express a need is improved by looking to the short term.

TO FINISH EARLY, START EARLY

When we have a firm deadline, the only way to add more time to our schedule is on the front end. For those of us who don't have a time machine, this might sound impossible. It isn't. With a little creativity and forethought, we can find many ways to "start before we start."

Part of the answer involves constantly playing and experimenting. If we always have a collection of sketches, notes, ideas, and prototypes in the works, we'll be ready to respond when a new request emerges. The idea is to proactively maintain (and continually refresh) a stable of material to draw from rather than waiting for a particular need to emerge. Maintaining a strong network of talented friends helps with this as well.

This is sort of like the scene in every Batman movie, where Bruce Wayne goes to see his head of research, Lucius Fox (played best by Morgan Freeman). Wayne has some new request, and Fox inevitably says, "Well, this project is *almost* ready . . ." It's almost ready because he started early.

The key word in all this is *playing*. Mr. Freeman's prototypes are not aligned against a specific, pre-defined need. They are explorations and investigations that may or may not feed in to some future system. They are ideas we pursue because they are interesting and might be practical someday. And they don't have to cost a lot. It's best if they don't. They just have to get the ball rolling.

The other way to start early is to leverage other people's work—with proper attribution and remuneration, of course. An example of this is what the military calls COTS, for "commercial off-the-shelf"—that is, buying existing components and putting them together in new and interesting ways. There is no great merit in starting completely from scratch, and it turns out we hardly ever have to do so. We can almost always start early.

DELAYS CAUSE DELAYS

A schedule delay increases the program's exposure to change, as new technologies, new threats, new people, and new economic realities conspire to place new demands on the project. Answering these demands takes time, and spending more time means we are exposed to even more changes. Thus the death spiral begins. The solution is to fight tooth and nail against any delays.

Parkinson's Law tells us that work expands to fill the time allotted, so adding time to the schedule easily becomes a self-fulfilling prophecy. When we have more time, we'll spend more time. Once the schedule begins to expand, the expansive tendency develops its own inertia and puts additional pressure against that final deadline. Keep this in mind when considering whether to extend a deadline.

A PROJECT LEADER'S INFLUENCE IS INVERSELY PROPORTIONAL TO THE BUDGET

An expensive project attracts more attention than an inexpensive one, and the more money we plan to spend, the more "help" we are likely to receive from various entities within the hierarchy. In contrast, smaller budgets correlate with autonomy; below a certain threshold the project simply does not appear prestigious enough, important enough, or risky enough to merit attention from senior managers.

COMPLEXITY IS NOT A SIGN OF SOPHISTICATION

Making something more complicated requires effort, not skill; there is a difference. The fact that we invested a million hours building a highly complex object does not mean we necessarily did good work. It just means we did a lot of work, which may or may not have been productive. In fact, a high degree of complexity probably means our work is not yet done.

A truly sophisticated design is one in which complexity is minimized. All unnecessary, ~~redundant, excessive, duplicative, duplicative~~ components are removed, and those that remain contribute positively to the object's objective.

Streamlining and trimming is a different kind of work than the more visible additive behaviors that make things more complicated, but this reductive work is just as important as the additive kind. Streamlining and trimming are what bring our design to maturity and ensure close alignment between what is built and what is needed.

A KICK-ASS HALF IS BETTER THAN A HALF-ASSED WHOLE

The phrasing for this particular heuristic comes from Jason Fried's book *Rework*. The idea is to be world-class at something rather than mediocre at everything.

FIRE recommends that projects advance through an iterative series of incremental steps, each of which provides a portion of the required capability and establishes a foundation for adding future capabilities as needs emerge and are validated. Trying to deliver a massive, expensive new project in a single step to full capability is the opposite of the FIRE approach.

On that note, our friends in the Agile software community tell us the delivery schedule should be prioritized, with the most important capabilities delivered first and the least important delivered last (or not at all). Listen to them. Don't put all the easy stuff up front. Definitely don't put the minor stuff up front. Pick the stuff that matters most and do it first. Then see what happens.

THE BEST WAY TO UNLEASH TALENT IS TO NOT HAVE TOO MUCH OF IT

This principle speaks to team size and recommends creating small teams of talented people. Large teams tend to dilute or even mute the talents of the members, thanks to the organizational version of the bystander effect, in which the mere presence of a crowd inhibits action and reduces people's feelings of responsibility. While the bystander effect is used primarily to explain why people in large cities do not render aid to victims of crime or accidents, in our case it illuminates the way otherwise talented, competent people fail to contribute in the presence of a large team.

People are less proactive when placed in large groups. They contribute less not only as a percentage of the overall effort but also in absolute terms. In a sufficiently large group, everyone does a little bit less than he would in a smaller group. Sociologists refer to this as *social loafing*.

Now, it's true what they say about none of us being as smart as all of us. Teams really are a good idea. But putting too many of us together at once can be counterproductive.

The secondary effect of the bystander effect/social loafing phenomenon just might be worse than the primary effect. In addition to discouraging people from expressing their talents and contributing to the current project, large groups also get in the way of talent *development*. People who don't contribute to today's project are missing the opportunity to hone their skills for future projects. The result is a workforce that is not only less proactive but also less well developed.

Social loafing has been observed in animals as well as humans, so it's a rather deep-seated part of us. Rather than trying to rewrite human nature or training people to overcome this ingrained tendency, FIRE suggests forming smaller teams in the first place as a way to maximize people's sense of responsibility and to encourage them to apply and grow their talents.

MINIMIZE THE DISTANCE BETWEEN
DECISION AND ACTION

The idea of reducing the distance between decisions and actions is a central theme of Peter Drucker's book *The Practice of Management*, in which he writes, "A decision should always be made at the lowest possible level and as close to the scene of action as possible." It echoes a similar concept from Catholic social teaching called subsidiarity, which asserts that things should be handled by the smallest, lowest, or least centralized authority capable of addressing that matter effectively. This concept was even adopted in article 5 of the Treaty on European Union as a way to manage intervention by the EU in various activities across the continent.

Subsidiarity means restraining not only the size of the organization but also the level of involvement in projects by people higher up in the organization. Relying on small groups of smart people and resisting constant organizational growth helps keep decision making close to the action and ensures that things are handled by the smallest possible competent entity.

THE TACTICAL ABILITY TO RAPIDLY DELIVER NEW
CAPABILITIES IS ITSELF A STRATEGIC CAPABILITY

In a brilliant 2011 report titled *Driving in the Dark*, former secretary of the Navy Richard Danzig recommends that the US Defense Department "build for the short term." He makes the case that in an environment of rapid change, long-term projects are a losing proposition. The future is opaque, so the further out we extend the time horizon, the more unpredictable changes will come our way. Danzig's recommendation to build for the short term is good advice even outside the realm of military technology.

Building for the short term is not a particularly new concept, but Danzig explains it better than most. His recommendation is not merely to build solutions in response to immediate needs but to foster and maintain a persistent capacity to rapidly deal with the changing demands of the environment. The idea is that constrained timelines allow for timely course corrections and prevent corporate sclerosis, keeping our products well aligned with the need. Thus, building for the short term does not mean focusing only on the short term. Our technology projects may be oriented toward the immediate, but our ability to consistently produce them is a long-term strategic strength.

The series of short-term solutions Danzig recommends would largely consist of iterative, evolutionary steps, each building on the lessons from previous projects. Some of these would be what Clayton Christensen refers to as "sustaining innovations" in his book *The Innovator's Dilemma*, while others would be the more explosive "disruptive innovations" that take us in an entirely new direction. Regardless of the flavor, these innovations would be focused on the short term but would have impact in the long term.

Naturally, sustaining innovations are more logical and easier to predict and produce. But by minimizing the investment—emotional as well as financial—in each project, the organization remains open to disruptive innovations, far more so than an organization that locks in long-term developments.

THE FUTURE WILL BE SURPRISING; PREPARE ACCORDINGLY

Building for the short term doesn't excuse us from doing long-term thinking, particularly because if we build a system that works and is widely adopted, it's likely to remain in service longer than anyone expected and will have to adapt to a changing environment. It is therefore important to build a responsive capacity for change into our systems.

We may not know what sort of changes will eventually emerge, but we can take concrete steps up front to mitigate the cost and delay associated with those unsurprisingly surprising changes.

In our exponentially interconnected world, this means we'd better make use of things like open standards and well-documented interfaces. Good systems engineering practices like "high cohesion, low coupling" help ensure that future changes to one component don't ripple expensively through the entire design. Modular designs, open architectures, well-defined interfaces—all of these help a system respond well to future changes.

Fortunately, open standards and modular designs do not have to be more expensive than their closed alternatives. In fact, the open approach might be cheaper in the short term as well as the long term, because it leverages design work that's already been done. But the real benefit is that it prepares us for the unexpected.

NO MORE THAN ONE MIRACLE PER PROJECT

When a product design relies on a large number of unproven, immature technologies, the opportunity for significant cost overruns and schedule delays becomes an irresistible force. Discoveries and breakthroughs rarely occur on a predictable schedule, so if a product requires several advances to occur before it can be built, we are setting ourselves and our customers up for disappointment. That is why former representative Heather Wilson (R-NM) advised that a program should aim for "only one miracle at a time."

Therefore, product designs should take maximum advantage of existing materials, components, pieces, functions, and ideas. We need to focus on building things we know how to build, using things we know how to use. A program might reasonably manage to bring one unproven technology or component to maturity, if that particular technology provides a critical function or important advantage, but attempting to deliver multiple miracles on a single project generally leads to excessive complexity, delay, and costs.

As the book progresses, watch for these principles in action. Some of them will be obviously and explicitly present. Others may require a bit of reflection to see how they contributed to the outcome. And in some cases, we'll see situations where the heuristic was not applied but should have been. We'll even introduce a new one or two. The more you train yourself to notice them—in their presence or their absence—the more useful they will be as reliable guides for your decision making.

Finally, a word of warning. These rules of thumb are shortcuts to wisdom, little Zen koans and iconic symbols hiding deeper truths. But not all heuristics are trustworthy or reliable. Beware the anti-heuristic, the shortcuts to foolishness, such as:

FASTER, BETTER, CHEAPER—PICK TWO
This supposedly self-evident guideline, sometimes called the Iron Triangle, seems rational and explicable. Countless practitioners and writers will enthusiastically explain

how improvement in two dimensions necessarily worsens performance in the third. Want it fast and cheap? No problem—but the final product won't be very good. Want it good and fast? All right, but it'll cost ya. The problem with this "pick two" idea is that it's not true.

Upon closer examination, we discover that what little data there is to support this position is largely of the nature of a self-fulfilling prophecy. We sacrifice one leg of the triangle because we believe we must, then look on our results as proof that the outcome was unavoidable. It does not have to be this way, and as Howard McCurdy explained in his book *Faster, Better, Cheaper*, NASA proved it could simultaneously improve the cost, schedule, and performance of a high-tech project. There's no need to pick only two.

YOU GET WHAT YOU PAY FOR

This silly little rule implies that we must pay a lot to ensure we get a quality product, as if a large price tag always correlates with quality. Excellence and expensiveness do not necessarily go together. As with the "pick two" idea, this rule of thumb tends to be self-fulfilling. It is certainly possible to pay a lot for a quality product, but throwing money at the situation is not the only way to achieve top-shelf results, and indeed it presents as many risks and problems as solutions.

TAKE YOUR TIME TO DO IT RIGHT

Here we find a suggestion that excellence correlates with a slow, cautious approach and an implication that extending the schedule will increase the quality of the final product. Yes, there is something to be said for taking the necessary time and refusing to inappropriately cut corners in the name of haste. But this guideline tends to point us in the wrong direction by taking too jaundiced a view of speed. It implies that speedy action is the antithesis of "doing it right," when in fact slowness puts us off course just as readily as excessive speed.

Clearly, some principles are more reliable and valuable than others. Discovering the difference requires a certain amount of experience and reflection. Spend some time listening to these guides and stay close to the ones that point you in the right direction, recognizing that the best heuristics are those that draw out our own wisdom and reinforce our best tendencies while illuminating areas where our natural inclination points in the wrong direction.

Speaking of the best, I've saved the best for last, and it comes from the final frontier. Actually, it comes from the fictionalized version of the final frontier known as *Star Trek*. Now might be a good time to mention that I wrote most of this book sitting at my dining room table wearing a blue Star Trek science officer bathrobe, just like the one Mr. Spock would have worn if we'd ever seen him in a bathrobe. Did I also wear a pair of customized, limited-edition pointy ears? I'd rather not say.

The FIRE Prime Directive

We begin in 1966, with the original TV series. When Captain James Kirk and his crew set out on their five-year mission to explore strange new worlds, they were guided by Starfleet's General Order Number 1, also known as the Prime Directive. First introduced in episode 21, "Return of the Archons," this rule prevented Starfleet officers from altering the natural progression of alien societies.

The Prime Directive was expressed in slightly different ways throughout *Star Trek*'s various incarnations, but the consistent idea is one of non-interference in alien societies, particularly those that are less technologically advanced. Now, Starfleet was clearly not anti-technology, nor was it averse to helping those in trouble, so its reasons for implementing this policy of restraint were clearly benevolent rather than Luddite or selfish. The Prime Directive aimed to protect new civilizations from suddenly being introduced to things like warp drive before they were able to grasp the implications and obligations that accompanied such technologies.

The rebooted *Star Trek: The Next Generation* series perpetuated the Prime Directive as it continued the mission of the original series. In an episode titled "Symbiosis," Captain Jean-Luc Picard explained the wisdom of the rule: "History has proven again and again that whenever mankind interferes with a less developed civilization, no matter how well intentioned that interference may be, the results are invariably disastrous." The not-so-subtle message is that introducing excessively advanced technology does not lead to good outcomes. That is true even for us today, which is why FIRE uses a similarly restrained concept. I call it the FIRE Prime Directive, and it states that project leaders may not interfere with the natural progression of a project by introducing unnecessarily advanced technologies or excessive, overengineered features. This directive applies particularly to immature technologies that have not been fully demonstrated in a representative environment (referred to as Technology Readiness Level 6 by NASA and military types).

The underlying idea is that immature technologies can

be unnecessarily complicating, expensive, or even destructive. Like Captain Picard exploring a new planet, project managers should refrain from introducing high-tech components where they don't belong.

Please don't misunderstand this as an anti-technology bias. Did I mention my *Star Trek* science officer bathrobe? Rather, the FIRE Prime Directive is an expression of restraint and focus, implemented for benevolent reasons and intended to benefit both the project's developers and the customers. It demonstrates an appreciation for the natural course of project development and suggests that interfering with that course is seldom wise.

It is perfectly fine to add a photon torpedo or warp drive to our design, but such additions should be organic developments in response to the project's objective rather than obligatory components of every single project. Note that Starfleet captains from Kirk and Picard to Kathryn Janeway (in *Star Trek: Voyager*) didn't prevent any planets from developing advanced technology. They simply refused to introduce warp engines where they didn't belong.

The lesson for us is to only add a warp drive to our ship if it needs to cross interstellar distances quickly. If we're building a short-range shuttlepod, an impulse drive is probably sufficient. Before my fellow Trekkies send me a flaming flood of e-mails pointing out how many Starfleet shuttles featured warp nacelles, let me emphasize I'm talking about sublight shuttle*pods*. Everybody knows the larger shuttle*craft* had warp drives. Duh. Also, it's possible those warp-capable shuttles might have been a wee bit overdesigned. Disagree? Send your complaints and corrections to Starfleet Academy, Department of Engineering, 1701 Warp Drive, Hollywood, California, attention Ensign Wesley Crusher.

Starfleet leaders instituted the Prime Directive because they understood the human bias toward interference and wanted to provide a counterweight to balance out our natural tendency. If people didn't have a track record of destructive interference, there would be no need for that rule. Similarly, the FIRE Prime Directive needs to be stated because the tendency of most engineers, designers, and project leaders is to continually inject new capabilities into our systems in the name of making them better. FIRE aims to shift our default position toward *not* including extraneous widgets, features, and functions, instead placing the focus on the fewest, most essential pieces. The reason for this emphasis on restraint is identical to Picard's—history shows us again and again that an overreliance on immature technologies causes disastrous delays, overruns, and complications.

But wait, there's a twist. While *Star Trek*'s Prime Directive sounds for all the world like a hard-and-fast rule, it was honored more in the breach than in the observance. In the episode "Flashback," Captain Janeway offered a mild critique of her predecessor Kirk, saying he was sometimes "a little too slow to invoke the Prime Directive." However, in "Equinox" she admitted that she too "bent it, on occasion." There is a lesson here for us as well.

In an episode titled "Justice," Picard said, "There can be no justice so long as laws are absolute. Even life itself is an exercise in exceptions." Thus, the FIRE Prime Directive should be understood as a general principle to which exceptions can be granted rather than an absolute rule never to be broken. Excessively strict enforcement of a rule tends to lead people to develop a large collection of loopholes that eventually lead to the rule never being followed at all.

It is better to have a flexible approach in the first place, so the rule can be applied where appropriate rather than disrespected and ignored even when it should be followed. This flexibility strengthens the rule by ensuring its application does not trump other operational necessities.

So it is with FIRE. On our projects, we should strive for a minimalist approach as much as possible, strenuously avoiding interference with the project's natural progression. But there will be times when, in the name of exploration and discovery, adding an immature component or advanced piece of technology is absolutely the right thing to do. And that's okay, so long as such divergences are done deliberately and with thoughtful consideration.

Just like in *Star Trek*, there should be some debate before bending, breaking, or otherwise violating the FIRE Prime Directive. There should also be some reflection afterward. We must bluntly acknowledge the deviation, at least to ourselves, and spend some time in self-examination, considering whether it truly was the right decision. This will help inform our future decision making. Might I suggest keeping your own version of a captain's log for just such a purpose?

There is a reason the FIRE approach is based on informal heuristics rather than rules, formulas, and checklists. These flexible little rules of thumb provide room for interpretation. They spark debate, discussion, and reflection. They are not designed to be treated as dogma, and they don't take themselves too seriously. It's pretty hard to take yourself seriously if you're wearing a *Star Trek* bathrobe and fake pointy ears. But just because we're not stoic Vulcans doesn't mean we're only goofing around.

And Now, Some Performance Data

Unless you skipped that part of the introduction, you already know the Condor Cluster was the fastest supercomputer in the entire US military when it was delivered in 2010. This single story proves FIRE can produce best-in-class results. However, one example only proves it *can* be done. We'll need to cast the net wider to show such outcomes are more than a fluke and that this approach correlates with excellence on a regular basis. Let's now consider a larger collection of performance data about products whose development story fits the FIRE pattern.

We begin with one of the coolest subgroups in the entire US military—Special Operations Command or, as its friends call it, SOCOM. Well, we're actually going to start with the nerdiest entity in the US government, the number-crunching Government Accountability Office (GAO), but they are writing about the Special Ops guys, so it's cool. Let me warn you now—there's a little math in the pages ahead, but I'll make it as painless as I can.

In a 2007 report, the GAO analyzed SOCOM's approach to developing new equipment, noting that "88 percent of the projects are relatively small, have short acquisition cycles, and use modified commercial off-the-shelf and nondevelopmental items." Military technologists refer to projects of this size as being in Acquisition Category III. To translate this into regular English, it means that 88 percent of the SOCOM projects are fast, inexpensive, restrained, and elegant. How about that!

In the interest of accuracy, I should point out the term FIRE is just a convenient way to describe the way they do business. It's my term, not theirs, so if you happen to run into a guy from SOCOM and you ask about his experience with FIRE, he'll probably look at you funny. Or he'll think you're asking about artillery.

Anyway, 88 percent of SOCOM projects fit the FIRE pattern. How did things work out? What sort of results did SOCOM get? Well, 60 percent of its projects stayed "within the original cost and schedule estimates." That's a significantly higher rate of programmatic success than most other organizations, military or civilian. As a point of reference, the Standish Group, a program management research firm, happily reported that success rates for commercial IT projects in 2013 were increasing, with 39 percent of the projects they examined coming in on time and on budget. The rate used to be much lower, but despite this progress in the commercial sector, it's still way below SOCOM's 60 percent hit rate.

The remaining 40 percent of SOCOM projects "experienced modest to, in a small number of cases, significant cost increases and schedule delays." Ah, maybe these Special Ops guys aren't so special after all, right? Well, if we keep reading we find that the "small number" of projects that came in late and over budget were "the larger and costlier" projects. In fact, the handful of troubled projects represented 50 percent of SOCOM's project funding. I believe the phrase you're looking for is "Mo' money, mo' problems."

Of course, the only thing this reveals is that the restrained approach tends to deliver on time and on budget, while the slower, pricier approach tends to be—well, slow and pricey. I mention it just to show that SOCOM is serious about minimizing time, money, and complexity on its projects, but let me remind us one more time: delivering on time and on budget isn't the real point. The goal is to deliver top-shelf gear, not just to keep the bean counters happy. Saving money is nice, but the real question is whether this approach led to effective new capabilities for SOCOM. Spoiler alert: it did.

One such project is the MG-47G, which transforms the venerable Chinook helicopter from a transport into an assault helicopter. In operations in Afghanistan, SOCOM's MG-47G proved itself an effective substitute for the UH-60 Blackhawk. In fact, a single MG-47G sometimes replaced upwards of five Blackhawks.

Other SOCOM projects had similar outcomes, performing brilliantly in some of the most difficult environments in the world. Clearly SOCOM's restrained approach to developing new equipment not only saves time and money but also ensures that it is the best-equipped, most effective force on any battlefield, anywhere in the world. SOCOM's superiority is in large part attributable to its members' training and character, of course, but having kick-ass gear doesn't hurt.

For a more comprehensive look at the performance impact of FIRE beyond SOCOM, we now turn to Pentagon analyst Pierre Sprey. In a 2007 presentation titled "Nothing's Too Good for Our Boys," he presented a series of "cheap winners" and "expensive losers," comparing the combat effectiveness of tanks, aircraft, rifles, and missiles. In each scenario, his data showed that the less expensive, simpler weapon outperformed the more expensive, more complex alternative. Sprey concludes, "Not all simple, low-cost weapons work . . . but war-winning weapons are almost always simple [and low-cost]."

I don't know about you, but all that weapon talk makes me itch a little bit. Let's change the subject to something a little more peaceful, shall we? How about computers?

Everybody likes computers. To use the more formal name, let's look at some performance data on "information technology systems."

As with SOCOM, we start by looking at the programmatic outcomes, the ability to deliver the requested capability on schedule and on budget. The Standish Group's 2013 report helps set the stage. The group summarizes its research findings thus: "In contrast to small projects, which have more than a 70% chance of success, a large project has virtually no chance of coming in on time, on budget, and within scope. . . . Large projects have twice the chance of being late, over budget, and missing critical features than their smaller project counterparts. A large project is more than 10 times more likely to fail outright, meaning it will be cancelled or will not be used because it outlived its useful life prior to implementation."

This is compelling data for anyone interested in delivering a new set of capabilities on time and on budget. And while primarily focused on the business side of things, the data illuminates at least one aspect of operations and usability. When a project fails to deliver or isn't used, I think we can safely conclude that its capabilities fall somewhat short of excellent. This does not mean every completed system is automatically excellent, but delivering *something* usually beats delivering *nothing*. Because FIRE projects have a smaller likelihood of failure than large projects, we've increased the odds of excellence. That's a good thing.

But let's go a little deeper. There are several quality metrics we could use to assess whether a project is any good. We could look at performance versus competitors, as Sprey did in his analysis. You'll recall that his conclusion was that superior gear tends to be simpler and less expensive, which suggests the FIRE approach correlates with quality. In a commercial context, we might instead consider "user acceptance rate," or calculate return on investment (ROI). The Standish Group's data suggests that this approach improves both user acceptance and increases ROI.

Before we move on to the next topic, we'll look at one final data set. These figures come from a tremendously awesome branch of the federal government, the only government organization I know of whose mission is literally to explore the unknown. I'm talking about NASA, of course.

In the 1990s, NASA launched an initiative known as Faster, Better, Cheaper (FBC). This approach focused on speed, thrift, simplicity, and restraint to deliver a portfolio of sixteen missions, which in aggregate cost less than the traditionally managed Cassini mission to Saturn. We'll look at these missions in more detail shortly, but for now we're just going to point out that FBC is entirely consistent with the FIRE model and observe that some of NASA's proudest moments of the 1990s were associated with these missions.

Specifically, the Pathfinder mission to Mars was scheduled to spend a month on the Red Planet. It lasted for three months. The *NEAR Shoemaker* spacecraft collected ten times more data than expected. And then there was the Stardust mission, which flew three billion miles to explore the tail of a comet, safely returned comet particles back to Earth, and then went on to help salvage a mission named Deep Impact. We'll take a closer look at Stardust in chapter 4.

These missions started out with tight budgets and short schedules, then delivered early and had money left over. That's good news, of course. Everybody likes it when the project stays on track. But the important part of the story is what happened *after* the launch, as these spacecraft boldly went where no one had gone before. In the final tally, FBC delivered ten successful missions for the price of the also successful Cassini, tackling some of the solar system's most challenging environments and answering questions that are literally cosmic. Ten for one is a pretty good return. It's even better when the ten includes a trip to Mars.

For all the talk about speed and thrift, FIRE is not really about saving time and money as a primary goal. See, if the final product isn't up to scratch, the fact that we stayed on budget and delivered on time is small comfort. The main goal is to produce world-class equipment, gear, products, and projects that perform brilliantly. The data from SOCOM, the Standish Group, and NASA suggest that FIRE does indeed correlate with excellent performance.

We cannot conclude that FIRE always succeeds (it doesn't), but we can safely assert that the method is capable of delivering best-in-class and first-in-class capabilities, sometimes both at once. This means we do not have to sacrifice quality or performance. Whether we're sending a helicopter to Afghanistan or putting a rover on Mars for the first time, FIRE can help us deliver a system that is affordable, on time, *and* absolutely world-class. Chapter 2 shines a light on how to find solutions that do exactly that.

Finding FIRE Solutions

A friend's Facebook post was slowly blowing my mind.

"Whoa, check this out," I told my wife. "Look at these tips from Lifehacker.com. They're so clever, so creative, and they are cheap and easy and—"

She laughed gently.

"Moms have known about these tricks for generations. They'd find them in the Hints from Heloise newspaper column."

"Oh," I cleverly replied, my mind blown for the second time in as many minutes. My feeling of deflation was temporary, replaced by new excitement.

"So all these futuristic techies who think they're learning some new life hack [I was speaking of myself, of course] are actually just rediscovering Heloise?"

"You're welcome," she replied.

Lifehacker's repurposing of old solutions for new audiences is not a unique situation. In fact, the rarity of unique situations is kind of the point. With nearly seven billion people on the planet today (and over 200,000 years since humans first appeared on the scene), it's pretty unlikely any of us will encounter a problem someone else hasn't already solved. This is good news. It means most of our solutions are out there, just waiting to be rediscovered and adopted.

When I began serious research into military technology, I discovered I was not the first to explore this particular territory. One of my favorite examples of a fast, inexpensive, restrained, and elegant success came from World War II. It starts with a letter from Karachi.

A Letter from Karachi

For anyone who finds aviation or military history even remotely interesting, the National Museum of the US Air Force in Dayton, Ohio, is a wonderland of wings, dreams, and engineering marvels. Visitors can get up close and personal with a replica of the 1909 Wright Military Flyer, featuring an engine donated by Orville Wright himself. Fans of Charles Schulz may want to check out an actual Sopwith Camel, which, much to my surprise, looks nothing like the red doghouse Snoopy flew in all those Charlie Brown comics.

The museum's Presidential Gallery contains a number of aircraft that once served America's chief executives, although the coolest object in that particular building is the non-presidential flying-saucer-shaped Avrocar prototype. Designed as a vertical takeoff and landing fighter-bomber, its top speed was an amateurish thirty-five miles per hour. Even worse, it became unstable at altitudes above three feet. The military was hoping to go a wee bit faster and higher than that, so in 1961, when it was clear that this thing didn't work, the Pentagon scratched it. But it looks really, really cool and, despite its limited flight profile, I want one so much it hurts a little.

Saucers aside, the real treasures are tucked away in the limited-access archives run by the museum's research division. No, I don't mean *real* flying saucers from Alpha Centauri. I'm pretty sure those are at the Dead Alien Research Facility on a secret base in New Mexico. The treasures I'm talking about are more down-to-earth.

I had the pleasure of examining some of these gems while visiting the museum a few years back. Entering the dimly lit archive warehouse feels like a scene from an Indiana Jones movie or, better yet, an episode of *Stargate*. Walking past partially dismantled stealth fighter cockpits, complete with dusty pilot mannequins, did not give me the willies at all.

At the risk of revealing the depths of my nerditude, I felt positively giddy when I sat down in a back room of the warehouse and a research assistant brought me a stack of boxes full of old documents, reports, and diagrams. This was not only because the room was well lit and the door was closed, so those creepy mannequins in flight suits couldn't see me anymore; the main reason for my excitement was the rare opportunity to peek into relatively unexplored corners of aviation history.

The generous and knowledgeable research staff did not disappoint. I devoured box after box of official documents, discovering artifacts and stories about airplanes and aviators I'd never encountered before. Not once did a mannequin come to life and chase me around the warehouse, which was both a relief and slightly disappointing.

One letter in particular stood out. It was dated August 26, 1942, and signed by Colonel Homer L. "Tex" Sanders, commander of the US Army Air Corps 51st Fighter Group. Colonel Sanders—apparently no relation to the fried chicken guy—was writing to the commanding general of the US Army Air Forces in India and China. The subject line simply read: "Fighter Airplanes."

This letter requested that the 51st Fighter Group "be equipped with P-51 airplanes as expeditiously as possible," explaining the aircraft's superiority in strikingly enthusiastic terms. He praised it for having "such perfect handling qualities as to put a smile of joy on the face of any fighter pilot." Colonel Sanders acknowledged that his assessment sounded "a little like flights of fancy," but he backed up his flowery language with hard facts and the clear-eyed opinions of experienced fighter pilots who had actually flown the plane.

For a fighter pilot, speed, range, and maneuverability are critical to survival. According to Sanders's letter, the P-51 Mustang provided best-in-class performance in all three categories. He explained that the P-51 was faster than the speedy P-38 Lightning even at altitudes as high as 15,000 feet. Citing three other contemporary aircraft, he stated that the P-51 "would easily outmaneuver a P-40, P-38 and P-66," and that its control "is perfect even at speeds of 500 mph." He went on to say it has "a range greater than any of the above tested aircraft," and pointed out that the pilots in his group who tested the P-51 "have been preaching it ever since."

Time would prove his assessment true. The US military went on to purchase 14,819 Mustangs, which would in turn fly 213,800 combat missions during World War II. After the war ended, the Mustang remained in service for thirty-five years.

At the risk of severe understatement, let me say that the P-51 was an outstanding aircraft. Certainly, Tex Sanders and his pilots thought so, and who would know better than they? Its record of excellence is cause enough to study it, but the reason it belongs in this particular book has as much to do with the way it was produced as with its combat record.

The somewhat apocryphal version of the P-51's development is that it was designed over a weekend, in a hotel, by a pair of engineers. Like most legends, that is not exactly what happened, but it is not terribly far from the truth.

Similarly, the widely cited figure of the first P-51 prototype being built in a mere 117 days is tempered by some fact-oriented historians who smugly insist the design work actually began three or even four months earlier. I would argue that the advance design work falls into the "to finish early, start early" category and would further suggest that debating when to start the clock is an unnecessary distraction. Also, even if we add four months to the 117 days figure, that's still a pretty fast project. The indisputable part of the story is that a relatively small team of smart people developed the P-51 quickly; it did not take years and a cast of thousands. Instead, speed, thrift, and smallness were held at a premium.

Similarly, the P-51 was a paragon of simplicity. Before writing about its smile-inducing qualities, Colonel Sanders praised the Mustang for being "an extremely simple airplane." Today such language may be seen as a criticism, but from the tone of the letter from Karachi, he clearly meant is as a compliment.

In addition to its ability to outfly the competition, Sanders praised the fact that the "engines, guns, radios, instruments and man[y] other parts are the same as those used on the P-40," which simplified supply and maintenance on the new aircraft. This was an important consideration given the 51st Fighter Group's austere operating conditions.

Colonel Sanders offered an interesting explanation for why his group was not already equipped with this clearly superior airplane. He reports a conversation he had with a senior officer from the Flight Test Section, in which the officer said the Mustang "didn't look like much so we haven't bothered much with them." This senior officer was expecting a more complex, sophisticated appearance and paid little attention to the modest-looking P-51. Apparently, looks can be deceiving. There's a lesson here for us all: you don't want to be the guy who failed to recognize the excellence inherent in a plane like the Mustang.

In an age in which it takes decades to design advanced fighter jets, and where the full fleet of F-22 Raptors consists of 187 jets, it is remarkable to read about the P-51's production rate. Sanders reports that the manufacturer, North American, was "building only 3½ per day." He quoted a company official's assessment that ramping up production to ten per day was possible, but it might take as much as three weeks to achieve this level of increased output. One can't help but feel something important has been lost since this letter was written, and that the efficiencies promised by high-speed computers and modern management methods have not quite been realized.

Colonel Sanders's letter is my favorite of the P-51 artifacts I discovered that day in the warehouse, but other commentators provided interesting information about the speed, thrift, simplicity, and restraint expressed in the production of this plane. A 1944 article in *Aviation* magazine even went so far as to describe it as "a plane that does not to any extent embody previously unknown engineering features, but rather employed refinements of known, accepted practices." Such a description would likely be seen as fighting words if used about a jet today, but like Sanders's comments about the Mustang's simplicity, this description was clearly meant in a positive tone.

What does all of this mean? First, it shows a correlation between excellence and speed, thrift, simplicity, and restraint. That is, we see that the premier fighter of its age was not the product of large budgets and long schedules, nor was it a highly complex aircraft. Note that it was not simple merely when compared to twenty-first-century jets; it was simple when compared to its own contemporaries, simple in the eyes of the grizzled colonel who wanted it so badly.

This suggests that excellence may not require expending decades and billions to build highly complex machines. It is possible to be fast, inexpensive, restrained, and elegant and still outmatch, outfly, and outfight all comers. We could do it in the 1940s. Maybe we could do it today, too.

This does not prove causality, but it does give the lie to any assertion that a high-performance device is necessarily expensive and complex and takes a long time to make.

On the question of causality, Colonel Sanders's words convey some hints that the P-51 is excellent *because* it is so simple, inexpensive, and rapidly available. For example, he complimented its simplicity, implying that being simple contributed to the plane's desirability and actively made it better than if it had been complicated. The P-51's simplicity also improved its maintainability, which is itself an important quality. And then there was the speed of production (ten per week!), which means it was available in sufficient numbers to make a difference on the field of battle. This does not merely correlate with excellence; it *drives* excellence, because in order for the aircraft to be truly great, Colonel Sanders and his fighter pilots needed a lot of them, and quickly.

The P-51's technical performance was unsurpassed. Its speed, range, and maneuverability gave it a huge advantage in a dogfight, while its simplicity, affordability, and availability ensured the advantage was actually realized. What we see then is not just a fighter plane that was great *and* fits the FIRE pattern. There is more going on here than just correlation. The P-51 was great precisely *because* it was developed quickly, inexpensively, and with simplicity in mind.

This means we have identified, at least potentially, a causal relationship between simplicity and superiority, between a tight schedule and a top-notch system. And where there is causality we may also find imitable practices. We may be able to re-create or copy some of the conditions and decisions that contributed to the P-51's outcome. Stories like this are at the root of FIRE.

And indeed, the contributing factors to the P-51's long reign as master of the skies are also found in a wide range of similarly superior technologies and products. As we will see in several stories throughout this book, the best stuff often has a constrained cost and schedule, has a low level of complexity, and is the product of a small team of talented, dedicated people working toward a tightly defined objective.

Whatever happened to Colonel Sanders, you might ask? He was eventually promoted to the rank of major general and in 1954 became commander of the Allied Air Forces in northern Europe. By the time he retired in 1959, he had received the Silver Star, the Legion of Merit, and the French Legion of Honor. Tex Sanders passed away in 1998, at the age of ninety-four, while living in Albuquerque, New Mexico. According to his official Air Force biography, Tex preferred the Southwest, calling it a place "where a man can drink a martini without getting his elbow jostled." I hope he enjoyed many unjostled martinis in the desert country he loved. He certainly earned them.

Special Operations Truths

Colonel Sanders wasn't the only one who discovered the value of being fast, inexpensive, restrained, and elegant before I did. In recent years, the guys who build gear for Special Operations teams also beat me to the punch and compiled a set of principles called "Special Operations acquisition truths," several of which sound remarkably like the FIRE guidelines I thought I'd invented. Jim "Hondo" Guerts, the SOCOM acquisition executive, put these truths into a widely distributed PowerPoint presentation, summarized below:

FAST does not equal UNDISCIPLINED

MORE BUREAUCRACY does not ensure a BETTER PRODUCT

RISK must be MANAGED NOT AVOIDED

FASTER does not have to increase COST/RISK

COMPETITION can be done QUICKLY

UNCONVENTIONAL THINKING is an ENABLER

CREDIBILITY AND TRANSPARENCY enable FREEDOM OF ACTION

Humans are more important than hardware

Quality is better than quantity

Special Operations Forces (SOF) cannot be mass-produced

Competent Special Operations Forces cannot be created after emergencies occur

Most special operations require non-SOF support

Despite the name, these principles aren't unique to Special Ops—they're just truths, one more example of someone else solving our problem for us.

It should come as no surprise to learn that even this pattern of finding preexisting solutions to problems has already been observed, studied, and documented. The practice of reuse is at the core of a technical problem-solving discipline known as TRIZ (pronounced *trees*).

TRIZ is a Russian acronym that, in translation, stands for theory of inventive problem solving. It was developed by Soviet inventor Genrich Altshuller and has been adopted by innovators around the world.*

One of the main TRIZ practices goes something like this: When faced with an unsolved technical problem, TRIZ practitioners translate the specific problem into a general problem statement, preferably in the form of a contradiction. They then consult a contradiction matrix to find general solutions to the general problem. All that remains is to translate a general solution into a specific application. Figure 2.1 shows the activity flow, beginning with the square at the bottom left corner:

For example, suppose we want to build a more powerful airplane. Increasing the engine size allows us to fly higher

---

* For more information, check out the TRIZ journal online at http://www.triz-journal.com.

and farther, because the larger engine has more power. However, the bigger engine also weighs more, which works against our effort to produce lift. Since the heavier engine simultaneously improves and harms the flight profile, we can state this as a general weight/power contradiction.

Consulting the TRIZ contradiction matrix reveals a number of different strategies for dealing with this situation. One such approach is called "anti-weight," in which we compensate for an object's weight by having it interact with the environment in lift-producing ways (i.e., buoyancy, aerodynamics, hydrodynamics). We might therefore compensate for a heavy engine by making the plane more aerodynamic, thus reducing the amount of power needed to push it forward through the air. We could also use lighter materials, such as aluminum or ceramics instead of iron. If the material itself cannot be substituted, we might be able to use a honeycomb lattice instead of a solid block of the material. The point is that several strategies are available.*

This approach saves time and money and minimizes rework by leveraging existing solutions. It also does something important: it forces us to understand the problem, and that just might be the biggest benefit of all.

It is easy to overlook this aspect of TRIZ, particularly if all we do is look at the diagram and nod, hypothetically agreeing that the approach sounds rational. To really appreciate the full benefits requires us to get our hands dirty. Once we put it into practice, we'll find that the translation from specific problem to general problem both requires and fosters a deep understanding of the problem itself. It may take a few iterations before this clarity and under-

---

* To learn more, check out an interactive version of the matrix at http://www.TRIZ40.com.

standing emerges, so despite the clean elegance of the four-step diagram, implementation and application is generally a bit messier than it appears.

That mess is more than okay. Time spent on understanding a problem at the beginning is quickly outweighed by the time saved in solving the right problem, particularly if we borrow the solution from a previous solver. Using TRIZ is a great way to turbocharge our problem-solving engines.

The heuristic is this: *Someone has already solved your problem.* The solution might be in an old Hints from Heloise column, a PowerPoint presentation by a Special Operations dude, or hidden away in some obscure corner of the Internet. The point is, it's out there; so find it, don't reinvent it.

Regardless of the approach or the specific tool, once we have a solid understanding of the problem, we can almost always find a preexisting solution. It's a big world, so discovering a unique problem for the first time is unlikely. If every candidate solution fails to make things better, perhaps the problem statement itself needs adjusting. This practice helps ensure that our understanding of the problem is pointed in the right direction.

Attentive readers may notice that this particular heuristic wasn't mentioned in the last chapter along with all the others. That's not a mistake. As previously explained, any list of heuristics is bound to be incomplete, so introducing a new heuristic in this chapter just reinforces the idea that we'll never have a comprehensive collection of every rule of thumb, and it discourages approaching that list as anything other than a starting point.

Finally, I should point out that TRIZ also loops us back to one of the most important heuristics: *To finish early, start early.* Sometimes the most efficient way to start early

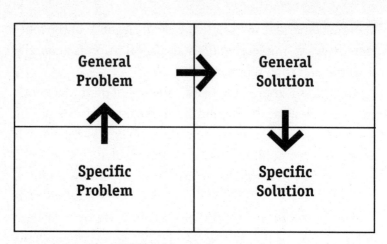

FIGURE 2.1. The TRIZ Problem-Solving Method

is to let someone else start early for you. But as the next story shows, sometimes we can start early without even realizing it.

If We Only Had a Wheelbarrow

The other day I had a meeting with a junior engineer—let's call him Bobby. The purpose of our meeting was to discuss his program's biggest problem and most high-risk item—the test schedule.

"We only get seven test flights," Bobby explained. "In order for our tests to be valid and to address all the requirements, we need more hours in the air. I don't think we can do it."

As we discussed a couple of strategies (more on those shortly), Bobby remembered an interesting piece of data he hadn't previously mentioned.

"Well, there will be a flight we call Flight Zero, so I guess we actually have eight flights." Sheepishly, he added, "And Flight Zero is probably going to be two flights . . . so that makes nine."

Looks like our friend Bobby had more flying hours than he initially thought. This realization didn't instantly solve all his problems, but it certainly opened up the realm of possible solutions. It also opened his eyes to the resources already at his disposal, which included roughly 28 percent more flight hours than he'd originally calculated. That's not nothing.

Our discussion reminded me of a scene in the best movie of all time, *The Princess Bride*. In this scene, the main character, Westley, is challenged to figure out a way to get into the castle and save his true love before she is forced to marry an evil prince. Like I said, best movie ever.

Anyway, Westley quickly concludes that the rescue is impossible. Given the time and resources available to him and his companions, there is no way to prevent Prince Humperdinck from forcibly marrying Princess Buttercup. Being a resourceful hero, Westley does not give up in the face of certain failure. He keeps thinking and develops a plan. The plan won't work, of course, because he does not have sufficient resources, but an impossible plan is better than no plan at all.

"If we only had a wheelbarrow," he muses. "That would be something."

His friends quickly inform him he *does* have access to a wheelbarrow. Maybe this story can have a happy ending after all (spoiler alert: it has a happy ending).

Here's the thing: we may not always have a wheelbarrow or a pair of extra test flights, but it is an absolute certainty that we have access to resources beyond the obvious. The key is to look for them.

I would now like to take a moment and apologize deeply to any readers who inadvertently agreed with that last sentence, because it's not true. I didn't mean to trick anyone—I wrote that line only to highlight a common misperception in the hopes that presenting the information this way will make it more memorable. Again, my sincerest apologies for the temporary deception.

Let me explain. Or, to borrow a phrase from another *Princess Bride* character, Inigo Montoya, "No, there is too much. Let me sum up." The part about always having resources beyond the obvious is true. But looking for them is not the key to finding them. Not at all.

You see, our hero Westley didn't find the wheelbarrow because he looked for it. Similarly, Bobby didn't discover Flight Zero and the Other Flight Zero by looking around. No, the first step in identifying these previously hidden resources was to express the *need* for them. Only then could the search begin.

Here's why this matters. As you may have noticed, the world is full of clutter. Extraneous data surrounds us; superfluous facts float hither and yon. Useless piles of detritus, however neatly organized, clamor for our attention despite their irrelevance to our needs. Looking at that junk isn't going to help us if we don't know what our needs are. There's a good change it would just confuse, overwhelm, and distract us.

Westley's breakthrough came when he announced that a wheelbarrow "would really be something." Until he arrived at the castle, understood his situation, and formulated a hypothetical but impossible plan, the wheelbarrow from two scenes earlier was just a prop, a bit of background scenery that didn't mean anything. The wheelbarrow only became "something" when Westley and his companions encountered a situation that required it.

Bobby's breakthrough was similar. He always knew about the pair of Flights Zero, but knowledge of their existence was stashed away in his mind along with a hundred million other facts about his project. Those flights did not have any mental meaning for Bobby until he expressed the desire for more hours in the air. It turns out he didn't need to tack extra flight hours onto the end of his schedule, because they were already there at the beginning. This allowed him to spend more time in the wild blue yonder without delaying the system's final delivery date.

Any creative problem-solving endeavor contains tension between reality and imagination. In Westley's case, he wisely began by confronting reality: his resources were severely limited, and time was short. His conclusion was that the rescue couldn't be done. Having accepted the reality of his unfortunate situation, he then entered a creative mental state that John Cleese calls the "open mode," which allowed him to imagine a solution that was impossible, given his wheelbarrow-free circumstances. The ability to imagine the impossible is a powerful ability indeed and should be carefully cultivated.

At this point, having developed an impossible solution, our hero discovered that his perception of reality was incomplete—a wheelbarrow was available after all. Thus the tension between reality and imagination was relieved not by limiting imagination to make it conform to reality but by discovering that reality already conformed to imagination. It bears repeating: we always have access to more resources than are apparent at first glance.

Previous comments notwithstanding, we should acknowledge that it is possible to find inspiration in a random jumble of junk, sifting through it without looking for anything in particular. We must be careful not to place too much emphasis on figuring out the solution before we look around. But let us also be mindful of the limitations of our ability to accurately observe the world. Yes, sometimes we don't know we need a wheelbarrow until we see it. But other times we honestly don't see it until we know we need it. I find this latter situation to be more common.

As promised earlier, we'll now take a look at a few of the strategies Bobby and I discussed that day. First was the idea that the key to finishing early is to start early. That concept is what reminded Bobby of Flight Zero, but it also points to a few other opportunities.

As is often the case with military technology programs, Bobby's contractor was going to test the hardware and software before handing it over to him for further testing. While there is value in repeating certain tests, it is sometimes possible to work together and use the initial test results to shorten the subsequent test schedule. Starting early doesn't mean Bobby himself had to start early. It just meant he had to widen his perspective on what constituted a start. Some of the best early work is done by other parties. Bottom line: Bobby was able to leverage some of the contractor's test results to shorten his own test schedule.

Phased testing strategies are not unique to the military, of course. Any development project tends to have a series of tests, some of which are redundant. There is nothing wrong with running multiple tests, and we often catch a problem on the second or third go-round that snuck past the first one. But these multiple tests also represent an opportunity to streamline and combine our activities, saving time and money while still ensuring that the project is rigorously examined.

The next strategy is to simply do less. Engineers in general (and test engineers in particular) have a tendency to conservatively overstate their specifications and their test plans. There are good reasons for this—and bad reasons as well. One of the bad reasons is a lack of focus and ill-defined priorities, which leads us to do more than is necessary.

Most new technology programs have a long list of features and functions. This is particularly true of airplanes, and it's entirely reasonable to want to test every single function before turning it over to a pilot—even a remote-control pilot. However, some functions are more important than others. Some are essential, others elective.

Whether resources are tight or not, it is wise to focus on testing the essential functions. Spending time and money on unimportant functional tests is not only wasteful but can also distract attention from the stuff that matters most and could cause us to overlook critical flaws. This means that streamlining in the name of speed and thrift can also improve quality.

Bobby needed to be able to identify his plane's most important functions and put his attention there. It is entirely possible he had more than enough time to perform the essential tests if he could just identify which ones those were. Further investigation showed that his test schedule only appeared to be inadequate because it included more than it needed to. In fact, a closer look revealed critical tests being crowded out by non-critical tests.

The third strategy is to fake it. No, not fudging the test results. I'm talking about supplementing flight tests with computer models and simulations.

There are limitations to this approach. As a NASA engineer once told me, the pipes never leak in the simulation, but they always leak on the launchpad. Because no model is fully accurate, live tests of actual systems are essential. But done well, a computer model can provide all sorts of data that would otherwise require a significant investment of time and money. Bobby was already planning some simulations, and we discovered opportunities to do more sims and thus reduce pressure on the actual flight tests.

Whether we're building hardware or software, for military or commercial purposes, anyone who says that a troubled project only needs more time and money is almost certainly on the wrong path. From a sheer problem-solving perspective, adding time and money is one of the least effective strategies around. Programmatically, such an expansive approach often overlooks the resources already at hand. Put together, that's a silly way to proceed.

In contrast, those who say that a project only needs a wheelbarrow are probably headed in the right direction. If they look around, they just might find the wheelbarrow was waiting for them all along.

Speaking of the right direction, chapter 3 considers some of the dynamics and mechanics that come into play when we use the FIRE approach. We'll see how to create the reverse snowball effect, talk about the nature and benefits of stability, and even take a look at how to get lucky.

FIRE Mechanisms

"We're late . . . again."

There's a reason those three words go together so frequently. In a maddeningly consistent dynamic, projects that are already late tend to experience additional delays. Projects that are already over budget tend to ask for more money. This should come as no surprise, because the same decision-making mind-set that leads us to try solving our latest problem by spending more time and money is precisely what puts us into that situation in the first place.

When the US Air Force's F-22 Raptor stealth fighter was finally declared operational in December 2005, it had been delayed many, many times since the program's inception in 1981. Nobody knows quite how many delays there were, but one of the first occurred in 1989 when project leaders extended the evaluation phase by a modest six months. Things went downhill from there.

Seven years after that delay, in 1995, the Congressional Budget Office (CBO) recommended canceling the long-suffering Raptor, calling it "both unnecessary and too expensive." They estimated the cancellation could save $14.5 billion over the next five years. This was a significant underestimation of the future cost and schedule.

The Raptor survived the CBO assessment and continued to expend more time and money in development. The first prototype flew in 1990, but it would take another fifteen years before the F-22 was declared operational. Finally, in 2005, the US Air Force was fully equipped with an advanced stealth fighter that could handle anything the Soviet air force sent our way. Too bad the Soviets had been gone for a decade and a half. I'm sure they would have been impressed.

Actually, "fully equipped" is too strong a statement. The original plans called for upwards of 650 Raptors. By 2009, after explaining that the jet had no role in the wars in Afghanistan and Iraq, the secretary of defense capped production at 187 aircraft. That's approximately 29 percent of the initially envisioned fleet, in case you didn't want to do the math yourself. As of 2013, despite US operations in Iraq, Afghanistan, and Libya, the F-22 had yet to fly a single combat mission in its first eight years of operational availability.

So much time, so much money, so little contribution to national defense. How did this happen? It turns out the F-22 was caught in a snowballing scenario in which delays caused further delays, which added to the cost, which increased complexity and delayed it even more . . . and that's just for starters. This had several negative implications for our nation's air service.

Because the thing was so expensive and was taking so long, it was essentially the only game in town. With so much money tied up into a single aircraft, all the hopes and dreams (aka requirements) of future capabilities rested in the Raptor's nest. This made it a prime target of opportunity—indeed, the only target of opportunity—for any additional missions Air Force leaders might want to accomplish.

Accordingly, this air-to-air stealth fighter was eventually given an air-to-ground mission and briefly redesignated the F/A-22 (A- being the prefix for attack planes). This added weight, features, and complexity to the plane, all of which meant that more time and money were needed. The F/A designation eventually went away, but the extra mission persisted.

A bomber version, called the FB-22, was considered but not built. Serious people with straight faces and nice ties talked about using this stealth fighter/attack jet to perform reconnaissance missions, although to their credit nobody proposed adding the reconnaissance prefix and calling it the F/A/R-22. Others suggested it could be used as a flying cell phone tower, an airborne communications node for soldiers working in difficult locations. Given enough time and money, surely a cargo mission could have added a C-prefix and an electronic warfare mission could add an E-prefix, resulting in a full-on F/A/R/C/E-22.

In the truth-is-stranger-than-fiction category, the Air Force got pretty close to this designation in December 2007, when Lieutenant General David Deptula said, "It's not an F-22, it's an F-, A-, B-, E-, EA-, RC-, AWACS-22. . . . It's a flying ISR [intelligence, surveillance, reconnaissance] sensor that will allow us to conduct network-centric warfare inside adversary battlespace from the first moments of any conflict in addition to its vast array of attack capabilities."

That's a whole lot of stuff to expect from a single fighter jet, particularly one that hasn't been allowed anywhere near the battle space.

The Raptor was designed to counter the Soviet air force, but all the budget overruns and schedule delays meant that the US Air Force did not get the F-22 until fifteen years after the USSR collapsed. For that matter, it didn't get much of anything else during that time frame either, because the F-22 was eating up so many resources. Rather than build a diverse fleet of specialized planes, the Air Force chose to build an aviation monoculture. Unlike an agricultural monoculture, the result was not bushels of cheap corn. Instead, the anticipated economies of scale never quite emerged; according to a 2013 Government Accountability Office (GAO) report, the Air Force ended up with a 71 percent decrease in quantity to go along with the 62 percent increase in program development cost.

Having apparently learned its lesson, the Department of Defense next pressed ahead with the joint strike fighter, a single jet to be used by the Air Force, the Navy, and the Marine Corps, along with the militaries of eleven other nations. It is on track to promise more, cost more, and take longer than the F-22 ever did. How well it will perform is anyone's guess, but if an underlying flaw is ever revealed, that flaw will impact pretty much everybody.

If we learned nothing else from Tom and Jerry cartoons, it's this: roll a snowball down a long hill, and by the time it reaches the bottom, it will be very large indeed. This snowball effect is exactly what happens in a program when we add time and money—and I'm not just talking about airplanes anymore. Whether the project is a software program, a military jet, or the next iPod killer, extending the schedule to accommodate changes, add functions, and fix problems means the program is exposed to more changes (of people, technology, budgets, and so on), which cost money to address and will require further schedule extensions. This exposes the program to yet more amendments and delays, and that can get expensive.

The more time and money we spend on the thing, the more complicated it gets, which in turn drives up the cost and schedule even further as we wrestle with all the complexity. Increased personnel turnover means less accountability and less learning; today's leaders are neither responsible for nor aware of yesterday's decisions and mistakes. Once we get into that cycle, it can be terribly hard to break out.

Fortunately, there is an alternative, a way to avoid or even reverse the accumulating layers of bureaucracy, the self-reinforcing delays, the institutional ignorance, the blame-my-predecessors unaccountability, the ever-expanding requirement list, and the commensurately expanding budgets. Two strategies for achieving the reverse snowball effect immediately come to mind: start with a smaller snowball, and roll it down a shorter hill.

Restricting the initial snowball size is critical, but hill length has the biggest impact, so let's begin there. Constraining the development timeline is metaphorically equivalent to using a short hill. A tight schedule presents fewer opportunities for additional layers to accumulate and thus minimizes the snowballing.

Rather than feeling pressure to incorporate every new good idea into the current design, project leaders can focus on delivering a restrained set of capabilities at the speed of need.

There are two dynamics at work here. First, a short timeline allows no room for the delays that naturally accompany adding new features. This helps constrain the system's complexity by minimizing requirement growth. Once the system is delivered, we may discover that the unadded feature wasn't really needed after all. If the feature is indeed necessary, the second dynamic comes into play: new features can be incorporated into the next system or the next upgrade—which is just around the corner, thanks to the speed and thrift of the first system. To continue the metaphor, we're rolling down a series of small hills instead of a single long one.

The decision to spend nearly thirty years building a fighter jet put the Air Force at the top of a very large hill. Any required capability had to be incorporated there, or it wouldn't be built at all in the foreseeable future. The result is a snowball of epic proportions.

Something else happened as the F-22 spent the better part of three decades in development. Something fast, inexpensive, restrained, and elegant. A metaphorical mammal emerged to occupy the environmental niches left empty by the huge, reptilian Raptor. That something was the unmanned aerial vehicle (UAV), now commonly called a drone.

Unlike the manned snowball, UAVs come in all shapes and sizes. With remarkable regularity and frequency, they fill in gaps on the battlefield and perform missions ranging from surveillance to communications to blowing stuff up with greater precision than ever before. For example, the Marine Corps' five-pound Dragon Eye surveillance drone gives forward-deployed troops eyes in the sky for roughly $60,000. Such smaller price tags (and shorter development timelines) have allowed for a greater degree of exploration and experimentation than the large manned platforms could accommodate. UAVs have also shown up in larger quantities, and their rapid development schedule ensures dynamic responsiveness and relevance to current needs and realities while simultaneously fostering rapid advances in the state of the art.

UAVs demonstrate the reverse snowball effect. Their smaller size and pilot-free simplicity enhance the speed and frequency of delivery, which in turn keeps costs down and frees up resources for other explorations. Because each UAV delivers *a* capability instead of trying to deliver *every* capability, the resulting environment is a diverse aviary of small, low-cost aircraft.

Anyone worried about economies of scale or diseconomies of diversity need only put the UAV environment alongside that of the F-22. It is immediately clear which approach is more economical. It is also immediately clear which approach delivers the most meaningful capabilities.

How can we apply the same dynamic to our projects? Start anywhere; constrain anything. Tighten the budget, and the schedule will constrict. Simplify the process and the architecture, and we'll see the cost drop. The virtuous cycle of the reverse snowball will take off automatically as long as we don't fight it. It works even better if we do it on purpose and help it along by following the full set of FIRE principles.

Virginia-Class Submarines

Despite all the talk about high-speed, low-cost projects, we can even achieve the reverse snowball effect in endeavors that are relatively large, expensive, and complex. That is because FIRE is not about the project's initial conditions;

it's about where we go from the starting point, no matter how high or low that starting point is.

Plenty of projects begin with short schedules and tight budgets, only to go on and bust both the calendar and the bank. Why is that? Because despite the project's humble beginnings, the project leaders decided to make things "better" by adding time, money, and complexity. That's the exact opposite of the decision-making pattern recommended by FIRE.

Other projects are large, expensive, and complex by any objective measure, and yet their leaders manage to minimize the cost, time, and complexity of their endeavor by applying these principles and tools to their project. This brings us to the topic of nuclear-powered submarines.

In 1995 Congress terminated the US Navy's Seawolf submarine program, even though it had a really cool name, citing a mismatch between the projected $33.6 billion cost for twelve submarines and the fact that the Soviet navy was not quite the threat it had been in the early 1980s when Seawolf began. Original plans called for as many as twenty-nine Seawolves, but the Navy ended up with three, at an estimated cost of approximately $4.4 billion each.

As so often happens on defense programs, the costs and delays had piled up significantly over the years. A 1993 report by the GAO calculated that "it will cost $683 million to design the SSN-21 class, which is 125 percent over the original contract cost estimate." Other aspects of the program had similar problems, so Congress decided to give the Navy what is known in military circles as "an opportunity to excel." In other words, they told the sea service to cut its losses and start over.

Of course, even though the Cold War had ended and the

Seawolf program was halted, the Navy still had a requirement to operate below the ocean's surface. They needed something much less expensive and less complex than the Seawolf. Thus the Virginia-class submarine program was born.

Let's skip straight to the punch line: in December 2011, the Virginia-class USS *Mississippi* was commissioned a year ahead of schedule and $60 million under budget. This was an impressive encore to the USS *New Hampshire*, which in 2008 came in eight months early and with $54 million left over. Prior to that, the USS *New Mexico* was delivered four months early, having required a million fewer work hours than its predecessor, the USS *North Carolina*—you get the picture. These continuous cost underruns came on top of an already reduced price tag, and in the final accounting each Virginia sub cost a bit under $2 billion, which as you recall is less than half the price of a $4.4 billion Seawolf.

Okay, you'd have to be a little bit crazy to look at a $2 billion nuclear sub and call it inexpensive or simple. And yet, within the context of this particular type of technology, the Virginia submarines just might be the fastest, least expensive, simplest, and smallest imaginable solution. When we put it alongside the Seawolf program, the Virginia program looks thrifty and speedy indeed. How did the Navy pull this off so soon after the Seawolf fiasco? How did it manage to deliver consistently early and under? Let's see.

From the project's start, Navy leaders set a new course for this endeavor. As Rear Admiral William Hilarides, the program executive officer for submarines, has explained, "The Virginia-class program . . . was originally designed with cost effectiveness in mind. In order to reduce costs on this program, we have to change the way we build submarines, and that's what we're doing."

This was not empty rhetoric. The Navy genuinely did things differently, beginning with a willingness to restrain the sub's requirements. For example, the GAO's 2011 report on selected weapons programs tells the story of a critical decision regarding the sub's electronics: "The Navy decided not to incorporate a conformal acoustic velocity sensor wide aperture array on the ship after it found it would significantly increase, not decrease, life-cycle costs and complicate maintenance."

You don't have to know what a "conformal acoustic velocity sensor wide aperture array" is to appreciate the fact that project leaders dropped a feature because it would increase costs and complicate maintenance. The technical term for that type of decision is *leadership*. Specifically, it is technical leadership, a willingness and ability to make engineering decisions based on a deep understanding of both the mission and the state of the art.

The Navy's Virginia team relentlessly pursued opportunities to make "capability neutral" changes to the design. These changes resulted in features that were less expensive, required less maintenance, lasted longer, and were less complicated to install, without reducing the boat's ability to do the job. One such feature was a "wet" sonar system instead of the pricier, more complicated sonar array used on other subs. Another was the payload integration module, which offered a modularized, mission-configurable weapons bay. This allowed the boat to adapt as mission needs changed, and reduced costs by $20 million per hull.

Why did the Navy follow this path? Not because any policy, regulation, or law required it. Instead, the project leaders genuinely believed it was important to be fast, inexpensive, restrained, and elegant, and they made decisions accordingly. They pursued speed, thrift, simplicity, and control at every opportunity, understanding that these principles would enhance not only programmatic performance (cost and schedule) but also the final product's operational performance. The result was a fleet of submarines that was not only delivered early and under budget, but also performed impressively at sea.

Let's look again at the GAO's assessment of the Virginia-class submarines. In what are perhaps my favorite lines from any government report ever, we learn that the Navy modified three critical requirements by making them less demanding: The original requirements, they determined, "were unrealistic and would not be worth the cost needed to achieve them." In addition, they noted, "the change will not affect operations."

I love everything about those two comments, but I'm particularly smitten by the second: the change will not affect operations. Obviously, changes like this make sense only if the resulting system can still get the job done. And indeed, the Virginia submarines passed their sea trials and are serving proudly today. Even if you're not in the submarine business, I suggest enshrining those two lines on a brass plaque, or at the very least on one of those yellow sticky notes, and posting them somewhere prominent. It is an example worth following whether you're writing software, building PowerPoint charts, or selling dishwashers.

Now, the Virginia-class submarines are not perfect. In 2010 they had a little problem when sonar-absorbing coatings sloughed off at sea, reducing the sub's stealthiness. I don't want to trivialize this situation, but I also don't want to make too much of it. The Navy resolved the problem in relatively short order, with minimal impact to operations. Such technical problems should not be taken lightly, but neither should they be treated as an indictment of the high-speed, low-cost approach to development. Similar problems regularly pop up in more traditionally managed programs. Spending more time and money on the Virginia subs might—*might*—have prevented this particular problem, but would have surely introduced any number of new problems, both technical and programmatic. As proof, allow me to direct your attention back to the terminated Seawolf program.

At the end of the day, the Virginia-class submarines offer compelling evidence for the feasibility of building high-tech stuff under budget and ahead of schedule. The Navy's experience shows that delays and overruns are not inevitable, and if it can do this on such a big, expensive project, surely the rest of us can do it on our projects as well.

The Virginia-class story also indicates the breadth of FIRE's applicability. Because FIRE emphasizes restraint, casual observers may conclude that the approach is only relevant to a certain class of simple problems, like portable music players or small software programs. However, the Navy shows this is not the case. The FIRE principles and practices can indeed inform our decisions on something as large and complex as designing and building a nuclear-powered submarine. This means that those of you working on megaprojects aren't left out—you too can reverse the snowball effect.

Stability
As Nassim Taleb has pointed out in *The Black Swan*, "The unexpected almost always pushes in a single direction:

higher costs and a longer time to completion." This suggests that surprising changes and program instability tend to trigger the snowball effect and cause us to bust the budget and schedule. FIRE provides a way for project leaders to inject stability across several fronts and helps minimize both the presence and the impact of the unexpected on our budgets and schedules.

Instability comes from many different sources, but the primary one is time. New discoveries and breakthroughs render previous technologies obsolete. Old competitors are defeated while new ones emerge. Political leaders come and go, as do program managers and project leaders. Economies expand and contract. Each of these changes impacts a project's structure, objective, funding, design, priority, and schedule. Our inability to accurately predict these changes contributes to the cost and schedule overruns that are so prevalent in technology projects.

Further complicating matters is the fact that a bad forecast only gets worse over time. A small forecasting error's impact can expand tremendously if it's left uncorrected. And let's face it, most forecasts aren't that great.

The importance of long-term forecast degradation was clearly seen in the F-22's story. During the twenty-six years the jet spent in development, countless technologies emerged and were replaced, requiring significant, costly, and time-consuming modifications. More significantly, between the project's start in 1981 and 2005, when it was declared operational, the Soviet Union collapsed and al-Qaeda emerged, dramatically changing the shape of the threat environment from what had been envisioned at the Raptor's inception. All these changes not only increased the Raptor's cost and schedule but also reduced its relevance to the point where the secretary of defense said, in 2008, that the aircraft did not have much of a role in the ongoing war on terrorism.

Whether we are designing fighter jets to counter the Soviet air force or working on the latest iPod killer, things are going to change. We cannot prevent these changes from happening. What we can do is limit the amount of change our project is exposed to, by moving things along as quickly as possible. So the first step in establishing stability is to move fast.

While speed gives a project a great deal of stability, a small budget also contributes—particularly if we're working within a large organization. When a large organization looks to save some money, a simple, low-cost project is not a very tempting target. If a project's budget is already small, it has essentially been precut, so further decreases are likely to be seen as not only unfair but unproductive and unlikely to make a dent in the organization's overall finances. Budget cutters are more likely to go after deeper pockets and larger projects that would better survive a reduction.

The combination of a short timeline and a small budget means the project is more likely to be fully funded from the start, rather than relying on budget authorities to authorize future (large) budgets. The short-term delivery schedule also means budget cutters are less likely to cut a current-year budget and promise to "repay" it with future dollars, since the project is slated to deliver before the funds can be repaid.

Finally, new regulations and corporate policies tend to focus on high-profile, big-ticket projects, because those projects tend to have the largest impact when they go wrong. Smaller projects with sufficiently small budgets can remain below the radar and thus minimize exposure to the unexpected changes that often accompany new regulations.

Simplicity also fosters stability, in terms of both technology and organization. Simple, mature technology tends to reduce the uncertainty and instability inherent in cutting-edge, not-quite-proven technologies. A simple design minimizes the number of interconnections, so changes are localized, with limited ripple effect through the rest of the design.

Organizationally, a simpler, more streamlined team tends to have faster and clearer communication than a large, complex one. This communication clarity reduces the amount of instability caused by miscommunication and bureaucratic inefficiency.

The bottom line is that FIRE helps projects present a smaller target to the forces of change, whether those forces are financial, technical, political, legislative, or in some other category. This does not mean these projects are more resistant to change. Rather, it means we are exposed to fewer changes in the first place, and are able to adapt to change more easily than a larger, more ponderous and slow-moving project.

On that note, my colleague, friend, and fellow Air Force officer Major Pete Mastro once offered an observation I've come to think of as Mastro's Law of Stability. He explained there is a difference between stable and static; while a static situation does not change, stability allows a system to *absorb* rather than resist change.

Pete points out that an aircraft in stable flight frequently changes its altitude, speed, or heading without becoming unstable. A stable aircraft moves and reacts to a dynamic environment, responding to the presence of winds, clouds, and other airplanes. This is a sharp contrast to retired planes mounted on pedestals for a commemorative "static display."

Instability in flight occurs when changing conditions (turbulence and so on) exceed the plane's ability to adapt. Stability means we can accommodate a changing environment while still making progress toward the objective. In the same way, the fact that FIRE fosters stability does not mean it prevents or avoids all change. Instead, it reduces the quantity and scope of change we must confront and helps us keep moving forward when the inevitable changes come.

FIRE reduces the bumps and jolts a program must respond to, but because turbulence is a natural phenomenon, it's easy to write off a smooth flight as merely luck rather than the product of decisions made by project leaders. Yes, there is an element of luck in all of this, but paradoxically it is a type of luck that is largely within our control. Let's take a closer look at the phenomenon of luck.

Wanna Get Lucky?

Successful program managers consistently describe themselves as lucky when they explain how they've managed to deliver some hot new capability despite having no time, no money, and a really small team. Maybe they are just being modest. Really, how many of us would actually brag to an interviewer about our own talents? Perhaps they attribute success to luck because they have no other explanation for why things worked out the way they did. Or maybe they really did get lucky. And if luck is a real thing, maybe there are steps we can take to increase our own luck factor.

Let's dig a little deeper and look at the words people use

when describing themselves as lucky. It typically goes something like this: "Mary had just finished up a project and so was available to join my team as the chief engineer. We were lucky to have her." Or, "We didn't quite know what we were doing, so we just tried some things and got lucky." Or, "We happened to find an existing technology that we could modify slightly and use on our project. How lucky was that?"

While the word *lucky* is useful shorthand to describe these situations, it turns out that the outcomes in question are not exactly random or unaffected by the decisions, personalities, or behaviors of the people involved. In fact, what appears to be luck may actually be something more than happenstance.

In his book *The Luck Factor*, Richard Wiseman proposes that luck production is to a large degree within our control. He identifies several common attributes of lucky people, including optimism, extroversion, low levels of anxiety, and openness to new experiences. He explains that people with these attributes don't win the lottery more often than their unlucky counterparts, but they do experience positive outcomes more often. The good news is that, with a little effort and imagination, these attributes can be learned and adopted by just about anyone.

Let's start with the relationship between extroversion and luck. Wiseman explains, "Lucky people score much higher than unlucky people on extroversion . . . meeting a large number of people, being a 'social magnet,' and keeping in contact with people." So in terms of sheer numbers, extroverts are more likely to know someone who can make a meaningful contribution to the project.

Extroverts are simply more likely to have a chance encounter with someone who can help solve a problem or join their team. So when we say, "We were so lucky Mary was available to join our team," what's really going on has more to do with mathematical probabilities than kismet.

This means our project manager wasn't just "lucky" that Mary was available to sign on as chief engineer. It's more accurate to say the project manager was extroverted enough to meet Mary, to stay in touch with her, and to strike up a conversation about the chief engineer position. If we dig a little deeper, we'll discover that the project manager had similar conversations with William, Bethany, Ivy, and Jenna. Talk to enough people, and we are almost guaranteed to find a person to fit that job.

Introverts take heart—you don't have to be the life of every party to get lucky like this. All it really takes is an awareness of the people around you and an occasional willingness to approach someone and ask if she might be interested in a particular project. Easier said than done for some of us, to be sure, so if you're on the far end of the introversion scale, you may want to consider partnering up with an extrovert from time to time, particularly when building a team or wrestling with a particularly thorny problem. I know that proposition sounds exhausting to some of you, but the lucky outcome just might be worth it.

The next component of luck is related to anxiety levels. Wiseman explains that "lucky people score much lower on neuroticism than unlucky people. . . . Because lucky people tend to be more relaxed than most, they are more likely to notice chance opportunities."

At first glance, the correlation between neuroticism and unluckiness might lead us to conclude that bad luck is the cause, not the effect. Woody Allen seems to think this is the case, but Wiseman suggests otherwise. His carefully constructed experiments show that anxiety and neuroticism obstruct our ability to take advantage of opportunities when they emerge. Passing up these opportunities minimizes the odds of achieving a lucky outcome, while pursuing them creates the appearance of luck. As the character John Nash said in the 2001 movie *A Beautiful Mind*, "My odds of success dramatically improve with each attempt." Again, what appears to be luck is actually math.

Next, Wiseman observes, "Lucky people score much higher on openness than unlucky people. . . . Lucky people have positive expectations about the future (optimism)." This openness increases people's awareness of emerging opportunities and makes them more likely to pursue—or even create—such opportunities. Similarly, optimism tends to correlate with a willingness to try new things, on the basis of a belief that the attempt will most likely turn out well. Ultimately, Wiseman argues that lucky people "create, notice and act upon" chance opportunities, resulting in what he refers to as "a network of luck" that sets the stage for positive outcomes in unpredictable circumstances.

Seeing the positive side of a bad situation has more to do with luck perception than luck production, but as it turns out, the very act of perceiving luck tends to help us produce it in future situations. People who get lucky tend to re-create the conditions that led to the desirable outcome. Statistically speaking, superstitiously wearing the same pair of socks every day isn't going to make much difference. But approaching the world in a relaxed, open, outgoing manner certainly will.

The good news is that while Wiseman writes about how personality factors like openness and optimism create luck, he also presents ideas on how a shift in behavior can increase one's luck. He describes simple exercises that can even be performed by an anxious, pessimistic introvert. These exercises might be easier for someone with a sunny disposition, but Wiseman's central finding is that personality is only responsible for luck to the extent that personality is responsible for *behavior*. Luck production is ultimately all about how we choose to behave, not whether we see the cup as half full or half empty.

This has implications for our projects and teams. FIRE encourages teams to exhibit the very personality traits and behaviors that correlate so strongly with luck perception and production. For example, constraining the schedule forces us to actively try things rather than endlessly study them. It builds in a bias for rapid action by removing a tolerance for delay and inaction. When time and money are short, we have to jump in and make an effort rather than wait until everything is perfectly arranged. This is precisely the sort of behavior exhibited by the optimistic, open-to-new-experiences people Wiseman studied.

Similarly, procrastination and neuroticism go together, while proactivity tends to correlate with a healthy openness to new experiences and a low level of anxiety. FIRE is nothing if not proactive, so when a team uses this approach it exhibits behaviors not unlike a person with a low neuroticism score.

A suitably constrained budget means we can't do things the usual way. When the obvious solution is not an option, the pessimist says it can't be done and therefore should not be attempted until additional funds are made available. The optimist, in contrast, recognizes the possibility of success and makes the attempt despite the challenging circumstances, thereby increasing the possibility of a lucky outcome.

People who are closed to new experiences and who have

a high level of anxiety are more likely to use process and policy as an excuse for inaction. They are more likely to be satisfied with continuing to increase the system's complexity, because reducing the complexity is a change in the way things have always been done (using a very narrow definition of *always*, of course). These anti-FIRE approaches correlate with unlucky outcomes. But people who are open to new experiences and have a low level of anxiety are more willing to abandon previous design behaviors and embark in a new direction, simplifying where they once complicated, doing more with less instead of doing less with more. That's what FIRE is all about.

FIRE encourages building small teams, which may seem to indicate introversion, but these small teams work best when they are part of a larger network of loosely affiliated partners, which is precisely the sort of thing extroverts are so good at building and maintaining. The number of people who are directly connected to the project on a full-time basis may be small, but the wider pool of talent that team draws from can be quite large indeed.

In summary, we see that FIRE nudges us in the direction of openness, optimism, and extroversion. It encourages our project teams to develop a personality that sounds a lot like the lucky personalities Wiseman describes. Those personality traits drive our behavior, and the result of that behavior looks a lot like luck. So if you want to get lucky, and I hope you do, then FIRE just might be your winning ticket.

And now it's time to strap in and put your space helmet on, because chapter 4 takes us into orbit—and beyond—as we take a closer look at some of NASA's finest missions.

FIRE Successes

NASA had a serious streak of bad luck in 1999. A series of four high-profile mission failures led to embarrassing headlines, such as the "metric mishap" in which inconsistency between English units and metric units led the *Mars Climate Orbiter* to miss the Red Planet entirely. Shortly thereafter, the *Mars Polar Lander* went silent during its final approach, apparently because its engines shut down prematurely. Public furor over these and other snafus led to the abandonment of the Faster, Better, Cheaper (FBC) concept under which NASA had been operating since 1992.

Unfortunately, NASA's early track record with FBC got buried in all the negative buzz in 1999, and for most of the world the concept devolved into the supposedly self-evident "faster, better, cheaper—pick two." However, there is more to this story than most people realize.

From 1992 to 1999 NASA launched sixteen major missions under the FBC umbrella, including five trips to

Mars, one to the moon, four Earth-orbiting satellites, and an asteroid rendezvous. In a remarkable demonstration of good luck, nine of the first ten missions succeeded wildly, including:

- The Near Earth Asteroid Rendezvous (NEAR), which made a two-billion-mile trip to intercept the asteroid Eros—the first time such a mission had been attempted. The *NEAR Shoemaker* spacecraft collected ten times more data than was expected, at less than two-thirds the original cost estimate ($122 million instead of $200 million). Despite not being designed as a lander, it gently set down on Eros's surface at the leisurely pace of approximately two meters per second. Undamaged, *NEAR Shoemaker* continued to transmit for two weeks. Its gamma-ray spectrometer was now a mere four inches from the asteroid's surface, increasing its sensitivity by a factor of ten compared to its in-orbit data collection capability.
- The Pathfinder mission to Mars, NASA's first attempt to put a rover on another planet, which weighed in at one-fifteenth the price of the 1970s Viking mission to Mars (in constant-year dollars) and was built by a team one-third the size of Viking's in half the time. Designed to last one month, Pathfinder lasted three months, collected 17,000 images, and was one of NASA's proudest moments of the decade. Pathfinder's achievements are all the more impressive, given Mars's reputation for eating spacecraft. In fact, despite nineteen attempts, the Russians ironically never reached the Red Planet.

Despite the initial string of triumphs, six out of sixteen FBC missions ultimately failed, which sounds like a high level of failure. However, it turns out the total cost for these sixteen missions was less than the cost of the non-FBC Cassini mission to Saturn. This means NASA earned ten wins for the price of one, an achievement that is underappreciated to this day.

How did NASA do it? It's a bit of a long story, but we could start with five of the unconventional secrets behind its underappreciated success.

1. Do It Wrong

As Alexander Laufer and Edward Hoffman explained in a 1998 report titled *Ninety-Nine Rules for Managing Faster, Better, Cheaper Projects*, "in order to do it quickly and right, the project team must be willing to do it wrong first." That's rule 18. The key is to undertake small, constrained experiments and build quick-and-dirty prototypes, most of which fail. This enabled NASA engineers to identify and discard impractical approaches, which eventually led them toward the right answers.

2. Reject Good Ideas

Each FBC mission focused tightly on a small set of critical activities, which meant project leaders had to say no a lot. For example, NEAR project manager Thomas Coughlin was flooded with numerous "good ideas" for new features, parts, and functions to add to his little spacecraft. He left most of them on the cutting room floor.

In Laufer's book *Project Success Stories*, Coughlin explains, "Had I incorporated even half of these good ideas, the spacecraft would never have been built. Only those changes that could be made with negligible or minimal disruption were even considered." The spacecraft's actual capabilities clearly exceeded its designed capabilities, as demonstrated by its soft landing on Eros.

Later projects were less restrained, which caused some of the aforementioned problems. As Howard McCurdy explains in *Faster, Better, Cheaper*, FBC projects tended to fail when leaders "reduced cost and schedule faster than they lessened complexity."

3. Simplify and Accelerate Everything

The focus on simplicity and restraint was not limited to spacecraft design. Engineers on the NEAR project famously used a twelve-line schedule to manage the project, and were fastidious about giving three-minute reports. In contrast, non-FBC projects tend to rely on hugely complex schedules that look impressive but can end up obscuring important activities. Similarly, long reports can create the illusion of communication, but a well-crafted three-minute report ensures that critical information does not get overlooked because the audience fell asleep.

4. Limit Innovation

Rule 61 from Laufer and Hoffman's *Ninety-Nine Rules* states, "Limit technological innovations and development to only those essential to achieve project objectives." This reflects the idea that it is better to ship a design that does *something* in real life than to design a ship that does everything on paper but never gets off the ground.

The most successful FBC leaders applied the concept to everything, including the definition of the term *better*. They held to the idea that a mission with one-half the capability is "better" if it performs the mission at one-tenth the price. This is a practical definition of what constitutes "betterness," and runs counter to the more-is-better mentality that typifies most high-tech development projects.

This approach had strategic implications for NASA. Limiting mission objectives a little saved a lot of money, thus making funds available for other projects. However, this did not represent a trade-off between cost and quality for the individual projects, as advocates of a "faster, better, cheaper—pick two" approach might think. Missions with limited objectives were actually more reliable, easier to test, and easier to operate. Fewer moving parts meant fewer things could break, and also limited the ripple effects of any design changes. This made the spacecraft more likely to succeed and ultimately delivered more than the sum of its parts.

5. Failure *Is* an Option

America's space agency is understandably proud of its rugged failure-is-not-an-option ethos, but under administrator Dan Goldin things were a little different. Goldin made it clear from the start: some FBC projects would fail. In fact, he said a 100 percent success rate would indicate NASA wasn't trying hard enough.

Of course, failures due to carelessness were not acceptable, but if a risky project failed due to the dynamics of exploring an unknown environment, that was okay. Such failures were tolerable in large part because time and money invested in each project were so limited. In fact, according to a 2001 report by the NASA inspector general, a major objective of the FBC approach was to "maximize the . . . amount of science obtained . . . while minimizing the impact of a failed spacecraft." Under FBC, failure was not just an option—it was expected!

After the unfortunate events of 1999, NASA launched several independent reviews to figure out what went wrong and make recommendations for future efforts. Since NASA stopped using the FBC approach by 2001, the investigators must have uncovered some intrinsic flaw in the methodology and recommended a new course of action, right? Actually, no.

The Faster, Better, Cheaper task force's final report, published in March 2000, emphatically stated that "Dan Goldin is right on with this FBC thrust" and talked about the need to "instill this cultural change throughout the complete organization." That is an endorsement, not a rejection.

The inspector general's report sounded a similar note, pointing out that the approach had been successfully implemented since 1992. The report recommended that NASA "fully incorporate FBC into the strategic management process." NASA management did not concur with this recommendation because it believed FBC was already sufficiently integrated in the strategic management process. Formalizing it would only suck the magic out and leave a worthless husk.

It's ironic; the practitioners who had successfully used FBC for years realized they could not continue doing so if they were forced to formalize the method. They knew it worked and regretfully abandoned it rather than see it become a complicated version of its former self. In contrast, the skeptics who did not believe in FBC recommended incorporating it into NASA's formal methods in the apparent belief that a method they believed to be ineffective would be much improved by bolting on a thick layer of bureaucracy. Everybody wins!

And so, despite its demonstrable effectiveness and emphatic endorsement by multiple independent sources, FBC went the way of the manned moon mission. Why? Certainly not because the data supported such a move. The most likely explanation—although exotic conspiracy theories about sabotage by aliens from Venus are way more fun to consider—is that four high-profile failures in a single year created irresistible political pressure for change and gave credence to shortsighted critics who had never liked or trusted the approach in the first place.

Regardless of the reason, NASA abandoned FBC in favor of a more expensive, complicated, slower approach to space exploration. By 2011 NASA had retired its space shuttle program, with no replacement in the wings, presumably because developing a new manned vehicle would take too long and be too expensive in the post-FBC era. Most of the rest of the world concluded that the Faster, Better, Cheaper initiative was a flop. But the truth is, FBC worked when it was tried. NASA actually figured out a way to pick all three. To see exactly how that happens, let's take a closer look at one of these successes.

Stardust

In 1999, NASA launched the *Stardust* spacecraft on an intercept course with the comet Wild-2 (pronounced "vilt-two"). Its mission: capture particles from the comet's tail and return them to Earth. As NASA's website explains, this was "the first robotic mission designed to return extraterrestrial material from outside the orbit of the Moon."

Reaching Wild-2 took five years. Returning the sample

took another two years, and when the sample return capsule hit the landing zone in the desert of Utah, it had traveled close to three billion miles. As a point of reference, Earth's circumference is roughly 25,000 miles, so the capsule covered a distance equivalent to 120,000 trips around the equator.

Stardust was part of NASA's Discovery portfolio (the official name of FBC), and it performed brilliantly in every dimension. When it launched—on time!—the project had more than a million dollars left in its account. The material and data it collected provided scientists with a bonanza of information about solar system formation, comet composition, and the environment of outer space. We also got some pretty cool technology out of it.

You can tell a lot about a project by the way the people involved describe it. Word choice can reveal the team's priorities, its design values, and its sense of what constitutes a desirable attribute. The Stardust mission page on NASA's website is full of rather intriguing language. The summary talks about "a simple spacecraft" with a "focused mission concept." It proudly claims membership in the Discovery series of exploratory missions, which were required to have a relatively low development cost of "less than $150 million." The introduction even mentions that Stardust's plan "was tailored to the schedule," which means delivering on time was a top planning priority.

Unpack those phrases and we find a project where speed, thrift, simplicity, and restraint were not merely tolerated but actively pursued and valued. Other programs may talk about delivering the most expensive, complex system ever, but Stardust makes a point of emphasizing all the ways the project expressed restraint. NASA set an aggressive schedule and tight budget, then actively pursued opportunities to spend less time and money. While no space probe is simple in an absolute sense, Stardust was definitely simple when compared with the alternatives.

These descriptions are not limited to the official online record. Ken Atkins, the Stardust project manager, kindly shared his experience and insights with me in a series of phone calls and e-mails. He repeatedly emphasized that being faster, better, and cheaper was fundamental to his mission's approach—and its success.

One of the ways Atkins constrained the costs on his project involved using equipment and components from previous missions. This thrifty approach helped reduce complexity, but it also led to some interesting challenges. For example, Stardust used a Motorola radio originally designed for the 1998 Mars Surveyor mission. The radio did everything NASA needed it to do, and its price fit Stardust's budget. Since Motorola was already building these devices, Atkins and his team were simply going to order the next one off the production line. So far, so good.

Unfortunately, the timing got sticky. The cash flow on Stardust's budget profile didn't quite line up with Motorola's production contract timeline, which called for closing the production line before Stardust funding was available to make the purchase. Restarting the production line at a future date carried an unacceptable cost increase, as did the idea of designing or finding a whole new radio. What to do, what to do?

Fortunately, the program manager of the Discovery portfolio had some funds left over from the remarkable NEAR project. Since both NEAR Shoemaker and Stardust were part of the same portfolio, NASA was able to slide some money over and gave Stardust a short-term, in-house loan so that Atkins could purchase the radio before the production line closed. He paid the loan back to the portfolio account the following year, when his funds were available.

While using mature, available technology is a good way to reduce complexity and costs, this story illustrates one of the dangers of this interdependent approach. When we rely on external sources for components, we are at the mercy of their priorities and timelines, which may or may not align with our own. It's all well and good if someone else's radio fits our mission profile, but only if the radio manufacturer is still interested in making that device when we need it a year from now.

The Stardust story shows us a way to handle that risk. When our project is part of a larger portfolio of similarly fast, inexpensive, restrained, and elegant efforts, there is a good chance that someone else will have finished early, with money left over, and together we'll be able to close the gap between needs and availabilities. And indeed, FIRE works best when applied to a portfolio of related projects rather than an isolated series of independent efforts. There is no guarantee that things will work out for us as nicely as they did for Stardust, but if you're looking for guarantees, maybe space exploration isn't for you.

Long before the *Stardust* spacecraft's launch, Atkins and his team set the stage for a successful mission by establishing and maintaining a tightly focused set of mission requirements. The primary science requirement was captured in a single sentence: "Collect 1000 comet particles > 15μm at encounter velocity < 6.5 km/s and return to Earth." This means the spacecraft only had to do three things:

1. Encounter the comet.
2. Collect a thousand particles.
3. Bring the particles home.

Easier said than done, to be sure, but this short list of three primary functions helped keep the team focused on actual needs and undistracted by secondary issues. Yes, Stardust had a three-tiered list of additional requirements, such as collecting interstellar particles, taking images of Wild-2, and providing in-situ particle analysis during the fly-through. There was even a further requirement: "Provide dust flux measurement of > 10^{-9}g to 1g particles." I have no idea what that means, but I'm sure dust flux is an important thing to measure. It's just not as important as hauling comet bits to Utah.

These second- and third-tier requirements are better understood as "desirements," in the sense of being desirable but not essential. This sense of priority helped the team orient its problem-solving efforts. Is the dust-flux-o-meter acting up? Okay, we'll try to get it working, but only if doing so doesn't interfere with our efforts to design the particle collector and doesn't make us miss the launch window. Is the camera resolution only 100 microradians (μrads) per pixel instead of the 67 μrads per pixel we mention in our secondary requirement? Get right on that, but first let's make sure the reentry vehicle will survive its trip through the atmosphere.

Atkins and his team had a particularly effective approach to defining requirements, using an exercise he called a "Capabilities vs. Requirements review" (CRR). In the CRR, they compared what they wanted the spacecraft to do with the capabilities of existing components. Atkins explained that this helped keep the project within its cost boundary by following in the machete-cut paths of those who'd explored the jungle before us. So along with the 1998's Motorola radio, the *Stardust* spacecraft also used a camera from 1977's *Voyager* (with a few upgraded electronics) and a computer from the Mars Pathfinder mission.

Keep in mind that the Stardust mission was a first-time attempt at a seriously difficult objective. It may have been built largely from existing components, but the resulting spacecraft was demonstrably first in class and best in class in terms of what it actually accomplished. And that's an important assessment.

All too often, engineers and other technologists like me assess the quality of a project in terms of how far it advances the state of the art instead of how well it performs in the field. We talk about building the "most advanced" system, as if what the customer really, really wants is advancement—whatever that means. A wiser approach is to focus on ability to do the mission, to provide meaningful capabilities. Who cares if the camera is twenty years old and the radio is borrowed, so long as the final product is awesome at doing something nobody has ever done before.

This willingness to use things already proven to work instead of insisting on building all new components is a key to Stardust's success and also a foundational FIRE concept. However, this does not mean we can never build a new component. It just means we should limit ourselves to no more than one miracle per project. For the Stardust team, that miracle was a tennis-racket-shaped particle-collection device stocked with a collection medium called aerogel.

Aerogel is a synthetic material with several interesting characteristics. It is 99.98 percent air by volume, making it the least dense solid ever created. The porous structure of this "glass foam" enables it to collect delicate comet particles that would be vaporized by a collision with a denser, harder object. Now, the first aerogel was produced in 1931, so it wasn't exactly a new discovery, but for this mission NASA scientists and engineers needed a particularly advanced aerogel. They created one with extremely high clarity and a variable density to ensure a soft catch that preserved each particle's entry track and didn't alter the captured particles in the process. This is harder than it sounds, but NASA made it happen.

Protecting the sample return capsule (SRC) during re-entry was another big challenge. At 29,000 miles per hour, the SRC's trip through the atmosphere was the fastest ever for a man-made object, roughly four times the return speed of any of the Apollo missions. To protect its precious cargo in such a demanding environment, the SRC rode behind a brand-new heat shield fashioned of a lightweight material called phenolically impregnated carbon ablator. It worked great, so maybe the Stardust mission relied on two miracles.

These two unproven elements (the particle collector and the heat shield) carried the most risk. The point is that Atkins and his team used known, proven components at every opportunity and only incorporated an entirely new construct when it was absolutely necessary for accomplishing the primary mission.

There is a second chapter to this story. After successfully delivering actual stardust to Earth and fulfilling all its mission objectives, *Stardust* was called into service one more time, to help mission controllers salvage a project named Deep Impact.

The *Deep Impact* space probe paid a visit to comet

Temple-1 in 2005, more than six years after *Stardust*'s launch. As the name suggests, this mission involved sending an impactor on a collision course with the comet, in the hope of revealing the comet's internal structure. It turns out that Temple-1 was rather dusty, and the collision produced a cloud of debris that blocked the camera's view of the crater, preventing NASA from collecting much of the data it had hoped for. Enter *Stardust* and its comet-capable camera.

Stardust had launched six years before *Deep Impact*, so chasing Temple-1 was never part of its flight profile. However, thanks to its efficient operations, NASA had enough fuel left over after accomplishing the main mission to arrange a flyby of the comet. The romantic little rendezvous occurred on Valentine's Day 2011, at which time the twelve-year-old *Stardust* took photographs of the six-year-old impact crater and revealed details the first probe had been unable to gather.

This unanticipated two-for-one bonus is a common outcome for projects like Stardust because simple systems built primarily out of mature, proven technologies tend to outperform their specs. That is, while a simple, low-cost product may be designed to do one thing, customers often figure out ways to make it do other things as well—things the designers never anticipated. This is a stark contrast to the tendency for expensive, complex systems to underperform and do less than they are designed to do. Just one more reason to pursue simplicity, thrift, and restraint.

Isaac Newton famously claimed to be standing on the shoulders of giants, a position the Stardust team also assumed. From that high perch, the team saw things no one had ever seen before and became a giant in its own right.

If we're wise, we'll follow the Stardust team's example and look for opportunities to build on the achievements of those who came before us. If we do it right, the resulting product just might provide a useful platform for those who follow us. Who could ask for anything more than that?

CHAPTER 5

FIRE Failures

Having looked at some successes, let us now speak of failure.

Developing new technology programs is a messy business. No matter how smart, experienced, good-looking, tall, or lucky you are, sometimes things won't go your way. Success is not impossible, but experiencing an occasional failure is inevitable.

The good news, according to French philosopher Roger-Pol Droit, is that when failure is certain, "any progress is of value." It's safe to say we can expect at least *some* progress mixed in with the inevitable failures. That's nice. Still, those pesky failures are what keep us up at night. Time for a closer look.

A central question on this topic is whether using the FIRE approach means we'll fail more often than the slower, longer, more expensive approach. The short answer is that FIRE fails less often, but the more nuanced answer points out that it depends on how we do the counting.

To illustrate, let's compare two hypothetical scenarios:

scenario A uses traditional methods and spends a million dollars over ten years to deliver a particular piece of equipment, while scenario B spends the same million dollars and same decade to produce a series of ten one-year programs. Scenario B's projects are smaller, and each one makes a more modest promise than scenario A's grand one, but for now let's assume the aggregate capability provided by scenario B is roughly comparable to the single step achieved in scenario A.

If the project in scenario A fails, we can calculate the failure rate as one failure per decade. That doesn't sound bad, right? We only failed once in the entire decade—yay for us!

Of course, we can also view it as a 100 percent failure rate over that time frame, which sounds somewhat less favorable. In contrast, let's say scenario B delivers only two successful products out of the ten attempts. In that case, we have eight failures per decade instead of just one, which is clearly (pardon my math) an 800 percent increase in the number of failures. Yikes! Somebody's gonna get in trouble!

On the other hand, it is only an 80 percent failure rate, which sounds pretty good compared with the previous 100 percent failure. So the question at this point is, which approach fails more? Again, the answer depends on how we do the counting and what we mean by "more."

Set aside for a moment the question of which specific projects failed and whether we should have said six out of ten would succeed instead of two out of ten,* or whether it's really possible to divide a large project into a series of ten smaller projects. Those are topics for another chapter. For now, let's focus on the question of which approach to counting our results is more meaningful.

---

* For what it's worth, the 60 percent success rate is more likely than the 20 percent rate.

Which scenario had a low rate of failure? Which had a high rate? If project A succeeds, should we chalk that up as a desirably perfect 100 percent success record or as an undesirably low rate of one success per decade? Both assessments are true facts, but maybe one way of framing the result is more useful than the other.

It is probably wise to be mindful of both calculations. You see, scenario B does indeed fail more often, in terms of the sheer number of failures we encounter over that decade. Tolerating an 800 percent increase in failure frequency takes guts. It takes imagination. It also takes elementary-school math skills. Sadly, these attributes are often absent from the corporate boardrooms where portfolios are assessed, and that's an important thing to keep in mind. Anyone who advocates using the FIRE approach will have to explain why he or she wants to adopt an approach that clearly fails "more often."

But scenario B also succeeds more often. For the same investment of time and money, we got two successful programs, not just one. Even though that sounds like a better outcome, treating the outcome like a batting average is still not a great way to assess progress. The key principle here is that there is no limit to the number of attempts we can make. There is only a limit to how much time and money we can spend. Since dollars and days are the limiting factors, they should serve as the denominator when we calculate our progress. Success per expenditure matters far more than success per attempt.

We're not playing baseball here, so don't get distracted by calculating a portfolio's batting average. If one team can make a hundred attempts using the same amount of resources that another team spends on a single attempt, it would be misleading to decide the first team performed less well because its attempts fail 50 percent of the time. The real question is what sort of successes it is able to deliver for the time and money it expends.

Consider this: we could argue that the aforementioned scenario A is actually one-tenth of a century-long portfolio that nobody will live long enough to actually witness. In contrast, scenario B's portfolio is visible on a human time scale, and that's important. The visibility of our outcomes means it's easier to learn from our experience and apply that learning to future projects. That's much harder to do on a single ten-year program, and the opportunity to learn from our failures is an important benefit of the FIRE approach.

Clever critics like to point out that producing a baby requires one woman and nine months. Nine women, no matter how hard they work, cannot obtain the same results over a single month. There is no flaw in this logic unless the intent is to argue that large programs can never be broken down into a series of smaller programs that deliver incremental improvements over time. In that case, the logic is entirely unsupported by reality.

As a general rule, dividing a large project into an iterative series of incremental steps is both possible and preferable. We might not be able to divide large projects indefinitely—at some point, we'll hit the equivalent of a nine-month gestation period—but we often do have the opportunity and ability to divide things up into smaller, shorter pieces.

In his book *Antifragile*, Nassim Taleb argues in favor of creating situations in which stress and negative outcomes cause improvements (these are "antifragile") instead of "fragile" situations, in which unexpected setbacks and challenges cause catastrophic results.

In our example, scenario A is fragile, scenario B is anti-fragile. That is, while we cannot predict with certainty whether project A will succeed or fail, we can determine the impact of its failure. It would hurt a lot because so many resources are involved. Similarly, in scenario B, we don't know for sure how many of the ten projects will fail, but we can tell that the impact of those failures would be contained.

Containing our losses is important, but that's not even the biggest advantage of the scenario B approach. In a portfolio of shorter projects, the opportunity to learn from failure is much greater than on the longer one. Each time a subproject in scenario B fails, it is a learning experience that can influence future decisions and enhance the outcome of future projects. That is the very definition of antifragility. In Taleb's words, when we have data-rich failures that teach us a lot, "every attempt becomes more valuable, more like an expense than an error."

There are two types of people in the world: those who believe things can be divided into two categories, and those who believe a binary approach is inappropriately limiting. I primarily think of myself as belonging to the second group, but nevertheless I would like to suggest we consider two types of failure: epic and optimal.

An epic fail is one that costs a lot and teaches a little. An optimal fail is the reverse—it teaches a lot and costs a little. Scenario A is a fragile situation, and when that project fails, it fails epically. A decade's worth of investment is gone, and the opportunity to apply the lesson to future projects is minimal. In contrast, scenario B is set up to be antifragile. When one of the smaller projects fails, it fails optimally.

The losses are contained, and the opportunity to learn is significant.

We may not be able to prevent every failure, but we can influence the direction in which we fail. By orienting our projects toward speed, thrift, simplicity, and restraint, FIRE makes us antifragile, increasing the odds of getting optimal failures and avoiding the epic fails. But sometimes FIRE is the very reason we fail, as we'll see in the following story.

The F-20 Tigershark

In the 1960s and '70s, an aerospace company by the name of Northrop had a big success with a little plane called the F-5 Freedom Fighter. A minimalist jet fighter, the F-5 offered affordable versatility and was adopted for front-line service by aviation units in over thirty countries. The US Air Force Thunderbirds aerial demonstration squadron once flew a variant of the F-5 called the T-38 Talon, in part because five Talons used as much fuel as a single F-4 Phantom, the Thunderbirds' previous airframe, an important consideration during the oil crisis of the 1970s. The US Navy's aggressor squadron still uses F-5s to simulate foreign jets in mock dogfights and exercises. We can safely say it's a pretty good little plane.

At a price tag of approximately $4 million per plane, the Freedom Fighter was almost a full order of magnitude cheaper than the highly advanced $30 million F-15 Eagle. It was the first fighter jet to incorporate the concept of "life cycle cost" in its design, which helped reduce the overall cost of ownership. But along with being cheaper to buy, fly, and maintain, the F-5 was surprisingly effective against the supposedly superior F-15, despite the Eagle's cutting-edge avionics and weapons.

An article in the *Chicago Tribune* from 1981 reported the results of a series of exercises called ACEVAL/AIMVAL—air combat evaluation/air intercept missile evaluation—held between 1975 and 1978. Over the course of a thousand engagements, F-5s went head-to-head against the much more expensive and advanced F-15 Eagle and F-14 Tomcat. Before the exercise began, computer simulations predicted the double-digit fighters would achieve a 70:1 kill-to-loss ratio versus the F-5. The overall ratio they actually achieved was 2.5:1. Some scenarios even resulted in a consistent 1:1 exchange.

Hang with me as I do a little math. For $60 million, in 1975 I could buy fifteen F-5s or two F-15s. Pit those asymmetric fleets against each other and, based on the 2.5:1 kill ratio, we should expect to see ten F-5s and no F-15s survive the engagement. Which side would you rather be on? Me, I think the smaller, cheaper fighter looks quite appealing.

Next, suppose we only buy ten F-5s and invest the savings into an expanded training program for our pilots. We would still have numerical superiority and might even see the 2.5:1 ratio drop further, based on the increased skill of the folks in the cockpits.

Some forty years after ACEVAL/AIMVAL, it would be silly to draw firm conclusions about particular air combat techniques or technologies. Although F-15s and F-5s are still flying today, the current versions are markedly different from those used in the late 1970s, so specific recommendations on optimal airframe selection would require additional tests, and that's not what this book is about. What we can observe in this particular instance is that the simpler system performed better than expected, while the complex one performed worse. While the ACEVAL/

AIMVAL results were controversial and interpreted in different ways by various analysts, even the most ardent F-15 partisan does not claim that the jet lived up to the performance predicted in computer models.

It is important to acknowledge that data points never speak for themselves. They must always be interpreted and analyzed to be understood, and there are several ways to interpret the ACEVAL/AIMVAL exercise. One inescapable conclusion is that the high-tech approach did not provide the promised dominant performance. This is troubling because dominance is the reason we undertake these big, expensive, complex projects in the first place. If spending all that time and money on a big complicated jet doesn't result in indisputable, unambiguous air superiority, maybe it's time to reconsider the approach.

Interestingly, some analysts looked at the ACEVAL/AIMVAL event and concluded that the F-15s obviously weren't advanced enough. Their proposed solution was to increase the cost and complexity of future systems even further, adding more features and functions to the Eagle to ensure that it would triumph in any future competitions. This reflects an a priori belief that such increases improve performance, even though the data suggests the opposite. Perhaps the F-15 designers would have been better off imitating the successfully simple aircraft instead of increasing the complexity of a plane already hampered by its own complexity.

Here's where things get strange and a little sad. By the end of the 1970s, buoyed in part by the ACEVAL/AIMVAL results as well as the F-5's worldwide popularity, Northrop decided to build a follow-on project called the F-20 Tigershark. Based on the F-5, the new Tigershark fit the FIRE pattern perfectly. Northrop's designers emphasized afford-ability from the start, since like the F-5 it was intended for sale to allied nations whose pockets were not quite as deep as Uncle Sam's. For similar reasons, the Tigershark was made simple; it was simple to operate and simple to maintain by military personnel who lacked the extensive advanced training of American forces. In fact, a pilot could qualify to fly the single-seat F-20 after just two days in the simulator. It required approximately fifteen hours of main-tenance for every hour of flight, far less than the thirty-three hours of maintenance required for each flight hour in an F-16 Fighting Falcon.

The Tigershark's operating range and the number of armaments it could carry were admittedly not as impres-sive as those of the top-of-the-line F-16s and F-15s flown by American pilots, though it had a much faster scramble time than the F-16 and overall was well suited to the actual mission needs of friendly countries like Venezuela and Pakistan. Besides, under the administration of President Jimmy Carter, exports of fully configured F-16s were not allowed.

The Tigershark's production timeline matched its scramble time. Northrop rolled out the first one in thirty-two months, a full month ahead of schedule. The strange, unhappy conclusion to our story is this: Northrop failed to sell even a single F-20. Nobody in the entire world bought one.

Here's why that happened: When President Ronald Reagan came into office in 1981, he reversed the Carter administration's restriction on foreign weapon sales. Sud-denly the Tigershark found itself competing in the mar-ketplace with the mighty Falcon. Sure, an F-16 cost twice as much and required more training and maintenance, but it's what the big boys flew, so it's the one everybody wanted. Never mind its price and complexity. Who cares that it was literally overkill, and actually less well suited to the more modest mission needs of our smaller allies. It was widely viewed as the best, so it's what everybody bought.

Under the Carter administration's restrictive export policy, the Tigershark would almost certainly have sold nicely and served well. Based on fifteen hundred test flights by Northrop pilots, the Tigershark was a reliable jet with solid performance. Since the F-20 was essentially an upgraded F-5, we might reasonably extrapolate the ACE/AIM results and suggest a fleet of F-20s would perform well against a more advanced opponent. But because none was ever sold, we can never know for certain.

Any product that sells zero units is clearly a failure, and the Tigershark sadly belongs in that category. There is no sense in denying it, although some from Northrop took to describing this project as "an R&D success" because it met or exceeded all the criteria for performance, reliability, maintainability, and operability. But it didn't sell, so the fiery little Tigershark was a flop. It was an informative flop, an educational failure worthy of our attention.

The first thing to recognize is that the Tigershark's losses were constrained. Northrop did not spend multiple decades and multiple billions of dollars on it, so the cancellation, while no doubt painful, was not fatal. Second, the failure was almost immediately evident. The F-20 was canceled quickly rather than having to endure a lingering, dithering demise.

It's tempting to attribute this failure to bad luck or bad timing. Had Reagan's election or the subsequent policy shift occurred a year or two later, Northrop would likely have been able to sell at least a couple of Tigersharks, and then with a foot in the door might have salvaged the program. But the timing was what it was, so rather than chalk it up to bad luck, let me freely admit that the F-20 failed because of FIRE.

The thing is, nobody wanted a small, simple, low-cost fighter jet if they could have a larger, more complex, more expensive one instead. There is a certain logic to this. Who in good conscience would send their pilots off to war in the second-best fighter? But there is also a flaw in this thinking, an unstated assumption that cost and complexity correlate to superior performance, or that the victor is the one whose airplane has the most advanced specifications. As the ACEVAL/AIMVAL exercise shows, that is not necessarily the case. Unfortunately for Northrop, the results of that exercise were not the determining factor in any nation's purchasing decision.

Let's be very clear: the Tigershark's limited performance was not accidental. In fact, Northrop was explicit and deliberate in its decision to sacrifice performance in order to achieve other objectives. As RAND Corporation researchers Tom Martin and Rachel Schmidt explained in a 1987 case study, "Northrop's export fighter program has been characterized by a consistent philosophy. In designing and developing an aircraft, performance must not outweigh cost, reliability, maintainability, and operability."

What is not clear is whether these less demanding specifications would have translated to combat losses. As the ACEVAL/AIMVAL tests showed, a larger fleet of less expensive aircraft just might win against a smaller fleet of pricier jets. Ultimately, hardware is seldom the deciding factor in conflict. What really matters is the skill of the person operating that hardware, and that is where the F-20's strategy made a lot of sense.

In his book *Outliers*, Malcolm Gladwell popularized the 10,000-hour rule, arguing that excellence is the result of practice and that spending 10,000 hours doing something tends to correlate with being very, very good at it. While the exact number of hours required to achieve world-class status may be subject to some dispute, there is no question that training improves performance.

Training also costs money, and pilot training in particular does not come cheap. Take the large number of classroom hours required, then add the fuel and maintenance necessary to keep the jets in the air; pretty soon we're looking at some big numbers.

The Tigershark aimed to reduce that burden, not only by making the hardware cheaper but also by emphasizing simplicity. Increased reliability meant a longer "mean time between failures," which made each aircraft available to fly more and cost less. The bottom line is that an air force equipped with F-20s would be able to provide its pilots with more practice and training for less money. More hours in the sky means more skill, and *that* is the deciding factor in almost any competition. In contrast, the larger price tag on an advanced jet like the F-16 meant less money was available for training and exercises.

Join me in a little thought experiment. Imagine a perfectly balanced hammer with an exquisitely ergonomic grip, a visually pleasing aerodynamic form, and a rigorously engineered handle structure that conveys the maximum force with minimal effort. It looks like no hammer you've ever seen, but the engineers assure you it is optimized for maximal nail-driving efficiency. Thor himself wishes he had a hammer like this one, and John Henry would be alive today if he'd had access to such an advanced piece of craftsmanship. Now imagine being gifted with this sublimely perfect tool and being invited to hammer a particularly important nail with it—a nail with global life-or-death implications. You count yourself lucky to have such a great hammer for such an important task. But then you discover the twist: you get just one swing. Good luck!

The hammer is up to the task, no doubt. It is a world-class hammer, a champion among tools. But who among us would feel confident in our ability to use an unfamiliar tool to its full effect? Wouldn't we instead ask to take a few practice swings, to develop a feel for the way this hammer functions? A master carpenter, already well versed in the ways of the hammer, might be more comfortable using this fancy hammer than I would, but I suspect even our hypothetical master would prefer to use a more familiar tool, one whose heft, structure, and function are already well known, thanks to years of use, not despite his expertise but because of it. This carpenter knows skill resides in the hand that holds the hammer rather than in the hammer itself.

The value of any tool increases with familiarity and experience, and human performance is as much a function of a well-trained mind as a well-designed tool. This is not to say that all tools are created equal; the one-dollar hammer you pick up at the local gas station's discount bin is almost certainly going to disappoint. But if the cost, complexity, and maintenance requirements of a tool reduce our ability to train and practice with it, that tool's actual utility is diminished, no matter how fancy and advanced it seems.

Nobody wants a "hangar queen" that spends so much

time being repaired that it never quite gets flown. Anyone unfortunate enough to own such a plane will be understandably reluctant to take it out for a spin unless absolutely necessary, which will have a derogatory effect on our pilot's readiness and skill. Bottom line: the customer is best served when the tools at hand are affordable to buy and fly.

This is why FIRE aims to reduce barriers to training, such as large price tags or ponderous maintenance requirements. By focusing on simplicity, we ensure that our customers can spend less time learning to use the system or maintaining it and more time actually using it. Similarly, a short development timeline puts the product in the field faster, so users can begin practicing with it right away. And keeping things affordable means users can dedicate some hardware to training missions without taking away from our operational obligations.

This produces an interesting quandary. On the one hand, simpler products with smaller price tags often outperform their more expensive, complex alternatives, in part because training matters more than hardware, and also because simpler systems tend to have greater reliability and are affordable in larger quantities. On the other hand, there is a widespread belief that the inverse is true and that superiority results from complexity. Make the system too simple and affordable and nobody will buy it, even if it really is better. What's a designer to do?

I'd like to say the solution to this problem is data, and for some people, it is. However, people's experience with one-dollar hammers that break at the first sight of a nail reinforces the already ingrained belief that "you get what you pay for." That belief can be hard to shake, even when results like the ACEVAL/AIMVAL exercises are readily available. It's even harder when such data is not around.

Northrop certainly found that to be the case. Despite achieving its technical and programmatic objectives on the F-20, it utterly failed to convince any buyers of the Tigershark's value. Its design approach fit the FIRE pattern perfectly, and the final product appeared to be exactly what Northrop was aiming to deliver. And still nobody bought one.

There is a lesson here for anyone who aims to use FIRE to develop a new product. It is not enough for it to be affordable, available, and reliable. It is not enough for it to be easy to use and maintain. It's even not enough for it to be demonstrably well suited to the customers' needs. If we produce something that is fast, inexpensive, restrained, and elegant, we run the risk of being completely rejected by customers precisely because they would rather have a more expensive, complicated product. It doesn't matter if they are making a good choice or not. It's their choice.

I won't insult your intelligence by offering a simplistic solution to this risk. Frankly, I don't think there is one. To be sure, we could talk about marketing and how to frame our project description so that it is presented in the best possible light. That's not a bad idea. Similarly, there is much wisdom in having a discussion with the customer in advance, when such discussions are possible. It's good to establish a common understanding between the developer and the user of the benefits of the FIRE approach. It is something to do *with* the customer, not *to* the customer. But the truth is, this risk exists; there's no getting around it.

As far as I can tell, Northrop did almost everything right. Then Reagan was elected, the world changed, and the Tigershark went the way of the dodo. I wish I could tell you that won't happen to you, but it might. It's something to keep in mind.

The other thing to keep in mind is that no approach is entirely risk-free. Spending a huge quantity of time and money on an enormously complicated gadget doesn't guarantee that people will buy it any more than the FIRE approach does. The Tigershark was a flop, but so were plenty of larger, more expensive, more complicated airplanes. The difference is that when the F-20 failed, it failed optimally instead of epically. Of course we would all prefer to win, and if this little jet had won, it would have won big. But since we are going to fail some of the time, we could scarcely do better than to fail like the Tigershark.

To continue the focus on failure, we now shift our sights from the sky to the ground and take a look at a prominent failure that appears to have used the FIRE approach but, unlike the Tigershark, had only a superficial veneer of speed, thrift, simplicity, and restraint.

The Division Air Defense Gun

Named after one of the most decorated American soldiers of World War I, the Army's M247 Sergeant York DIVAD (Division Air Defense) gun was a self-propelled antiaircraft weapon developed in the early 1970s. It looked like a tank but performed like a turkey, and was canceled in 1985 after gobbling up $1.8 billion and the delivery of sixty-five wholly inadequate vehicles. In a fine demonstration of the military's capacity for irony, after proving incapable of shooting down aircraft, most of the DIVADs went on to serve their country as stationary targets on Air Force bombing ranges. Inexplicably, a few of these failures were placed on public display, including one in Tennessee's Sergeant Alvin York State Historic Park, much to the chagrin of US senator Jim Sasser (D-TN), who asked that the project be known solely as DIVAD rather than Sergeant York, out of respect for his state's prominent World War I hero.

At first glance, the DIVAD program had all the appearances of a FIRE project. For example, the Army planned to develop the system in less than seven years instead of the typical ten to fifteen years. The project manager, Colonel Russell Parker, told the team he expected "a much reduced development time, thus resulting in an earliest fielding date." This is precisely the sort of guidance one would expect to find in a program being developed according to FIRE principles.

The aptly named Brigadier General Nelson J. Cannon similarly affirmed the Army's commitment to thrift, explaining that "the paramount evaluation factors were system performance and cost." The DIVAD was to be primarily assembled out of existing, mature components with a proven track record and known functionality; this approach was intended to save time and money while also minimizing complexity. The Army seemed quite intent on leveraging speed, thrift, and simplicity in its pursuit of this new gun.

Unfortunately, this approach did not produce the expected results. In a series of operational tests, the DIVAD was unable to hit its flying targets if they maneuvered from side to side. No problem, said the Army as it programmed the target drones to fly in a straight line. When this predictable trajectory still proved to be beyond the DIVAD's capability, the Army brought in hovering targets. Next, it added a radar reflector to make the targets easier to spot. Then another reflector. And another. And—surprise—another, for a total of four. Attempts to convince the Soviets to add multiple radar reflectors to their aircraft were unsuccessful, as were requests that Soviet forces limit their aerial activities to hovering.

The test results were not complete failures, of course. In one test, the DIVAD successfully shot down nine out of eleven targets, which made lots of people happy even though an 82 percent hit rate is still a bit on the low side. Upon closer inspection, we discover that several of the targets had to make multiple passes so the DIVAD could score a hit. That made lots of people less happy.

Shall we do a little math? Although the actual figures are not available, let's conservatively assume that fewer than half of the eleven targets made one extra pass each, for a total of five additional passes. The DIVAD then would have a hit rate of nine out of sixteen, or 56 percent, instead of 82 percent. The actual rate was almost certainly lower.

In another scenario, the DIVAD mistakenly locked onto a latrine near the test range, apparently misidentifying the latrine's rotating fan as a low-flying helicopter. Since the enemy rarely attacks using combat latrines, this was considered an undesirable feature. These underwhelming test results convinced the secretary of defense to cancel the program and send the ignominious results to the bombing ranges.

Let's take a look at what went wrong. Early on, the developing contractor was allowed to trade off requirements for cost and schedule savings, because speed and thrift mattered more than being high-tech or high-performance. So far, so good. This is actually a smart idea, and is precisely the sort of thing FIRE recommends, because overvaluing advanced technology tends to drive delays, costs, and complexity in the wrong direction while simultaneously introducing all sorts of performance problems caused by working on the bleeding edge of technology. We really are better off building an 80 percent solution instead of continually chasing the elusive 100 percent solution. However, upon closer examination we find that these trade-offs were not thoughtful, productive decisions and did not deliver the necessary results. Instead, they made things worse. Right idea, wrong execution.

You see, the DIVAD team had an aggressive timeline for delivery (as we all should), but the primary strategy for staying on schedule was to ignore performance problems. Oops! In 1988, Army Major Michael Ditton wrote a piece for a journal titled the *Army Lawyer* in which he explained that "greater priority has been given to adhering to the schedule than to correcting some serious system performance problems." In retrospect, I think we can all agree that failing to fix the system's problems is a crummy way to stay on schedule. We might even say that failing to fix the problems means we didn't stay on schedule at all.

In 1987, John Adams published an article about the DIVAD in the Institute of Electrical and Electronics Engineers' *IEEE Spectrum* magazine in which he explained that the contractors "unveiled their prototypes on schedule"; he then went on to observe that these prototypes "were unexpectedly immature." The phrase "unexpectedly immature" seems to indicate a significant degree of incomplete work, which begs the question of whether something should be considered "on schedule" if it is not completed on time. Personally, I think that failing to complete the work by the delivery date is the precise definition of "not on schedule."

Pardon me while I get all philosophical for a moment. If a tree falls in the forest and crushes a prototype that did not exhibit the expected level of maturity when it was delivered, wasn't that prototype behind schedule? Because, you know, it was not finished on time? Truly, this is a question for the ages.

Or maybe it's an easy one to answer. The contractor delivered a fraction of a prototype, so the unfinished portion represents the degree to which it was behind schedule. Adams used the phrase "calendar schedule compliance" to describe the situation, which sounds suspiciously like saying the program was on schedule because June successfully followed May. However, flipping over a new page on the calendar does not mean we're on time, even if we flip everyone's calendar all at once. The fact that it is June for the whole team only means that time has passed. Being on time would require flipping the calendar *and* getting the work done. So while FIRE encourages project leaders to trim unnecessary activities, the DIVAD project apparently skipped the entirely necessary part about building something that functions correctly. The end result was, as they say, less than optimal.

Similarly, Major Ditton's article says project leaders "successfully controlled costs" on the DIVAD development, a dubious assertion given the system's persistent immaturity. I would suggest that project leaders merely controlled *spending*, not cost, which is a horse of a different color. That is, they spent as much money as they'd planned to spend, but what they produced was far less than their customers needed. In simpler terms, if I'm planning to buy ten apples for a dollar and I spend that dollar to purchase only five apples, my fruit actually costs twice as much per bite as originally budgeted. I may be controlling my spending in that situation, but I haven't controlled my costs. This is where the DIVAD calculation went wrong. Rather than an inexpensive *solution*, the project leaders settled for an inexpensive *program*, which is not the same thing.

Organizationally, the Army made a well-intentioned attempt to simplify the procurement process, largely freeing the contractor from the complexities of government regulation and requirements. The company was not subjected to all the typical layers of government oversight, which everyone agrees is a good idea. However, it appears the Army overcorrected because its otherwise admirable hands-off policy was accompanied by a less virtuous eyes-shut and ears-plugged stance. In hindsight, we discover there is a difference between not interfering with the contractor's decisions and not being aware of them.

While the DIVAD experienced plenty of structural and organizational problems, what really sank its boat were bad technical decisions. In the name of thrift and simplicity, the DIVAD borrowed several components from other military projects. Again, this is precisely the sort of design behavior FIRE advocates, based on the idea that someone has already solved most of our technical problems, as well as on the principle that mature tech tends to be cheaper, simpler, and more reliable. What the DIVAD team failed to understand, however, is that this approach is only effective if the technology selected for integration into the system actually does what it needs to do.

Since the DIVAD was a heavily armored tracked vehicle, the Army decided to use the same chassis as that of the M48 tank. This sounded like a good idea at the time. The problem was that the DIVAD weighed sixty tons, while the M48's 750-horsepower engine was only capable of hauling around a fifty-ton tank. Since the DIVAD's weight exceeded the engine's designed capacity by 20 percent, it had a tough time moving from place to place. Because of the mismatch between what the DIVAD needed and what the M48 chassis provided, one might argue that the selected component was not really a proven component and was not appropriate for this purpose.

The same thing happened with the target tracking radar. In an admirable sign of multiservice cooperation, the DIVAD borrowed a radar system from the US Air Force's F-16 Fighting Falcon. Just as the M48 chassis was a poor fit for the DIVAD's actual needs, the jet fighter's radar proved to be ill suited to the mission. The radar was originally designed to track fast-moving targets from a fast-moving platform. In contrast, the DIVAD was trying to lock onto slow or stationary targets from a platform that moved quite a bit slower than a fighter jet. So all the things the radar was good at were all the things the DIVAD did not need it to do.

The DIVAD story reminds us that applying the FIRE principles requires a certain amount of thoughtful nuance. It is not enough to set a firm deadline and deliver your prototype on time; the prototype has to actually work. It is not enough to simply integrate a bunch of existing components; those components have to actually be capable of performing the necessary functions. And it's not enough to hit a stationary target that's been augmented with multiple radar reflectors unless you can convince your opponent to put those reflectors on their aircraft as well.

That failures happen should come as no surprise. We've all been there. The question is what to do when we're heading for a brick wall, and the next section offers an answer for how to deal with certain types of failures.

The Clark Rule

I don't like being told what to do, and in keeping with the Golden Rule, I try not to tell anyone else what to do either. It is therefore with a certain amount of trepidation that I break form to offer this very concrete, very specific prescription for your consideration: *Cancel any project when its cost growth exceeds 15 percent.*

I probably mean that very much. If a project overruns its budget by 15 percent, it's almost certainly on a trajectory to overspend even more, so do us all a favor and nip it in the bud before things get crazy. For that matter, you may want to start sharpening the ax when cost growth hits 14 or even 13 percent. If you can't cancel the project yourself, then make that recommendation to whoever does have the authority. Better yet, put words to that effect in the contract, so the termination option is clearly spelled out from day one. You won't regret it.

Hard and fast rules like this are not exactly my forte, but I stand behind this one with confidence. Well, mostly. I also trust that my dear readers are too wise, clever, and well groomed to interpret this rule too strictly. Yes, yes, it might be okay to keep going if your program's cost growth hits 16 percent, but don't say I didn't warn you.

And no, I'm not talking about a situation in which your product is such a success that the customer orders 15 percent more of it so you have to hire more people or buy more raw materials. That's not the type of cost growth I'm talking about. But you're a smart person. You knew that already.

Where did this 15 percent figure come from? What's

the basis for this rule? To find the answer to those questions and more, journey back with me to a simpler, gentler time, a time when business travelers could bring a bottle of water onto an airplane, before Facebook, MySpace, or even Friendster (kids, ask your parents). Come with me all the way back to the previous century, to a year known as . . . 1998.

With the Y2K bug still ominously lurking in the future and NASA's *Lunar Prospector* safely orbiting the moon in a soon-to-be-successful search for lunar water, leaders at America's space agency pulled the plug on a project to build a remote sensing satellite named *Clark*.

Clark was a companion to the doomed *Lewis* satellite, which burned up in orbit due to a design flaw in its attitude control system. Apparently even NASA forgets to carry the 1 sometimes. But *Clark*'s cancellation was different from *Lewis*'s spectacularly flaming descent. NASA leaders canceled the project for one simple reason: its cost growth broke the 15 percent threshold.

While *Lewis* was on time and just slightly over budget, *Clark* was two years behind schedule and had overspent its $50 million budget by 10 percent even though it wasn't finished yet. It was on course to spend a total of $62.5 million, so project executives hit the kill switch to prevent that from happening.

Commentators at the time described this as a blow to the famous Faster, Better, Cheaper (FBC) initiative, which until that point had racked up an impressive 90 percent success rate. I see it differently. Canceling *Clark* actually demonstrates FBC's effectiveness, not its failure.

Usually, canceling a government project like *Clark* is a long, painful process implemented only in response to delays and overruns of epic proportion. Even after it is clear to all observers that the project is irretrievably broken, cancellation still takes forever, costs a lot, and is strenuously resisted by an assortment of special interests ranging from Congress and lobbyists to the leaders of whatever agency was responsible for the program. *Clark* was different.

Like all the low-cost missions in the Discovery portfolio, *Clark* was built on a promise of a termination linked to that 15 percent growth point. This established both a clear expectation and a legal mechanism, ensuring that all involved parties were aware of what would happen if the project spent too much money.

In reporting the cancellation, *Science News* called it "a long-awaited decision." In other words, everyone saw this coming. This is a stark contrast to the more typical shocked and surprised reaction that comes when a project gets canceled for being over budget and behind schedule.

For example, the Army canceled its Comanche helicopter program in 2004, citing excessive delays and costs. As he made the announcement, the Army deputy chief of staff, Lieutenant General Richard Cody, admitted, "If you told me six months ago that I would be standing here saying the Army no longer needs the Comanche helicopter, I wouldn't have believed you." Would that all leaders were so forthright.

The Army no longer needed the Comanche for many reasons, including the changing nature of the battlefield. But a main reason for the shift in need was the Comanche's ballooning cost. By some accounts, Comanche was on track to consume 40 percent of the Army's aviation budget. Who needs that?

Lieutenant General Cody admittedly did not see this

coming, but the contractor was even more surprised. Despite having spent twenty-two years and $6.9 billion on a helicopter that was supposed to have begun flying in 1996 but was still imaginary in 2004, a spokesman for Boeing issued a statement that Comanche was "on track and schedule" one day before the Army announced it was terminating the project. To quote the great Forrest Gump, "That's all I have to say about that."

In hindsight, it seems clear that canceling Comanche was a good idea. Any time you spend two decades and multiple billions trying to build something but fail to even settle on a blueprint, it's probably time to step away from PowerPoint and reorient yourself. For that matter, it might have been smart to cancel Comanche *before* entering that death spiral. If only the Army had instituted the Clark Rule and canceled Comanche when its cost grew by 15 percent! That would have been a much happier ending to that particular story.

Signs of trouble were certainly present before 2004, but Comanche continued anyway, in the apparent belief that the best way to fix an overspent project is to spend even more. In their defense, this approach is hardly unique to Army aviation.

Let me be clear—good idea or not, canceling a little project like *Clark* is hard. Canceling a big project like Comanche is even harder, because we all have a natural tendency to view sunk costs as a reason to keep going. The larger the sunk cost, the less likely we are to walk away from our "investment" (aka "loss"). To date, the best economists in the world have been unable to prevent the vast majority of us from falling victim to the sunk cost bias, and I have no intention of tilting at that particular windmill. What I will do is suggest that establishing plans, agreements, and expectations in advance makes it easier to do the smart thing when confronted with mounting losses. We may still struggle at the thought of walking away from an unfinished project, but it's much easier to do so if this course of action doesn't come as a total surprise.

There is never a bad time to make a good decision, but the best—and easiest—time to do so is at the beginning. By creating unambiguous incentives and consequences, we help ensure that expectations are clear to all involved. According to McCurdy's *Faster, Better, Cheaper*, NASA leaders "had promised they would terminate any project that incurred cost overruns. When the *Clark* satellite broke the 15 percent barrier, NASA executives did not wring their hands and rescue the program with additional funds. They canceled it, just as they said they would do."

That promise was critical, as was their determination to keep it. It is a brilliant example of integrity and technical leadership. It is precisely the type of promise we should all make—and keep—in each of our endeavors.

When a project starts to go off the rails, by all means we should make an attempt to salvage it. But at a certain point we really are better off cutting our losses and trying something different. NASA decided that 15 percent cost growth represented their pain threshold, and it's not a bad standard. But whether we pick 10 percent, 20 percent, or 13.2 percent (see, I told you hard-and-fast rules aren't my forte), it is wise to have a specific trigger that causes us to reassess our trajectory. It is also wise to pick the trigger point *before* the project begins, to put it down in black and white, to make the promise and to mean it.

Clark does not have a particularly happy ending. There

is no surprise twist, no final bit of good news. NASA did not launch *Clark II* from its ashes. The satellite named after one of America's greatest frontiersmen and explorers was simply canceled, and that was that. Yes, some components and technologies from the project were retained and made available for other purposes, so it was not a total loss, but there is no sense in polishing the turd. *Clark* was a failure.

While the project clearly failed, it also demonstrated an important strength of the Faster, Better, Cheaper initiative. Specifically, it showed the will and ability to stop a project before its costs hit the stratosphere. NASA leaders made a promise and kept it. They made the tough call. The right call. It is an example worth following.

Speaking of making the tough call, we now turn our attention to an ancient Greek puzzle that has become a modern metaphor for complexity: the Gordian knot.

CHAPTER 6

Cutting the Gordian Knot

The best part about serving in Afghanistan was the opportunity to work alongside soldiers, sailors, airmen, and marines from so many other nations. The small team I led during my brief stay was made up of officers from five different countries, and I variously reported to generals from Italy, Germany, and France in addition to my American commanders. In keeping with the fine tradition of militaries traveling on their stomachs, I ate waffles with the Belgians, had maple syrup with Canadians, and enjoyed a surreally delicious duck à l'orange in the French general's dining facility. I even sampled a tin of military rations from Croatia, but frankly I preferred the French cuisine. I'm sure my Croatian friend, Major Srecko Gojic, understands.

The Macedonians were a particularly fascinating group. They frequently invited me to drink their thick Macedonian coffee and spoke proudly of their homeland at every opportunity. One day, while I chewed my way through a particularly buzz-inducing cup, they informed me that the historical figure I know as Alexander the Great goes by a different name in Skopje. His modern descendants refer to him as simply "Alexander the Macedonian," presumably because *great* and *Macedonian* are synonyms in their native tongue.

I mention Alexander the Great Macedonian because of the way he dealt with the fibrous labyrinth known as the Gordian knot. For those unfamiliar with the story, the short version is that he untangled this famously complicated bit of macramé by slicing it in half with a sword. This act signified his qualification to become king of Asia based on a conveniently retrospective prophecy.

That's pretty much the whole story, although the way my Macedonian friends told it gave me plenty of time for a second cup of coffee. Fortunately, I wasn't planning to sleep that week anyway.

As an American, I never quite subscribed to monarchical government structures, so my opinion on qualifications for becoming royalty is woefully uninformed. Therefore, whether or not Alexander's solution made him suitable to be king is a topic I'm entirely unqualified to address. Purely as a matter of personal preference, I suppose I would rather have a decisive king with creative problem-solving skills like Alexander than a royal who dithers and ponders and gets all tangled up in the intricacies of intractable problems like Hamlet, but all the same, I prefer to vote for my leaders.

Anyway, the thing to understand about the Gordian knot is that it was opaque. The outer layers obscured the inner bends and twists, preventing even the most skilled knotsman from visually comprehending the situation. It didn't matter how rigorously Alexander and his advisors measured, weighed, or mapped the knot—its core retained secrets untold.

While no one could possibly comprehend the complexities within this enigma of entanglement without an as-yet-uninvented X-ray machine, the man who would be king nevertheless perceived a solution. He realized that untangling the knot did not require a PhD-level understanding of the knot. The fastest, most effective, and most direct route to the center of that tangle was to use the edge of his sword.

Alexander's problem-solving strategy is alternately praised for being innovative, simple, and effective and criticized for being brutish, thoughtless, and violent. I'm inclined to agree with the first assessment rather than the second, and not just because my Macedonian friend was such a good storyteller. Even before hearing his version of the tale, cutting the Gordian knot already made a great deal of sense to me, at least in terms of solving that particular problem. It always seemed to me that the point of the untangling was simply to untangle it rather than to preserve the Gordian twine. Cutting was therefore a perfectly reasonable approach. Of course, if the string itself had some particular value, then cutting it might be a bad idea, but that does not seem to be the case.

Now, the last thing in the world I would want to do is interpret this story as a metaphor to justify the use of military force instead of diplomacy, although no doubt many have done so. Instead, I choose to see this as a story about successfully reframing a problem and metaphorically cutting through the distracting ephemera surrounding a long-standing puzzle. Where Alexander's contemporaries assumed the integrity of the Gordian twine had to be preserved, Alexander realized the knot itself was the problem to be solved. Where others assumed a complex problem required a complex solution, Alexander realized the best way to confront complexity is with simplicity.

When we are confronted with a modern version of the Gordian knot, we would do well to consider Alexander's example. The first step is to examine our assumptions and make sure we are focused on solving the right problem. Are we supposed to untie the knot in order to produce a long string, or is it sufficient to simply do away with the knot, in which case we may be able to sacrifice the string? In general terms, we might ask if a complex situation genuinely requires a complex solution, or whether simpler approaches could serve perfectly well.

All too often we hold to an unstated and unexamined assumption that complex problems require complex solutions, or that the best way to deal with excessive levels of complexity is by throwing more complexity at them. When we expose such assumptions to the light of day, they tend to crumble. Yes, any given situation will have a certain degree of unavoidable complexity, but we can and should aim to get as close to that minimum as possible.

A modern example of Gordian knottiness is the amount of paperwork and the number of reports, charts, and graphs used by program managers to track, assess, and explain their programs. This tangle is generally produced to support all the very important oversight performed by managers in large organizations. Let's take a closer look.

Oversight

If you've ever worked in, with, or near a bureaucracy, you know that the one single thing bureaucracy loves best is meetings and reviews and oversight and reports and assessments and score cards. And PowerPoint charts. And templates. And checklists. And more PowerPoint charts.

Wait, you didn't really think there would be only one thing on that list, did you? It's a bureaucracy we're talking about here. Of course their one favorite thing is almost a dozen things. I originally planned to only have three items on the list, but the twenty-person down-select committee tasked with streamlining the original four items decided to add a few instead. There was nothing I could do about it.

Anyway, one of the most frequently mentioned barriers to implementing FIRE in a large organization is the crushing level of bureaucratic oversight and management reviews foisted upon innocent project teams. We're not talking about an appropriate level of due diligence, a well-advised audit, or an occasional short briefing to keep the boss informed on the team's progress. There is no reasonable objection to that type of monitoring. No, we're talking about something much more severe.

What I object to is dedicating the entire project team to a four-week review whose sole purpose is to explain why the five-year-long project had a one-day schedule slip. Same goes for passing through eighteen layers of redundant assessments by people who are fundamentally, psychologically, and organizationally incapable of making a decision before finally being allowed to talk with the actual decision maker, or holding a million-dollar meeting to make sure the research and development budget saves ten bucks this year. And yet these things happen.

Case in point: Frank Kendall is the top acquisition and technology executive for the entire US Department of Defense. In an April 2013 speech introducing a new government efficiency initiative, Kendall shared a true story

about the time he received a briefing from a program manager. Kendall asked a couple of follow-up questions. These
questions required additional research, but the program
manager, being a clever and resourceful chap, was able to assemble all the answers within an admirably quick forty-eight
hours. Unfortunately, he then had to spend three full months
going through all the various reviews and coordination steps
before he was allowed to present the requested information
back to the boss. In his speech, Kendall made it quite clear
that this was not how things are supposed to work.

Of course, this sort of thing is not limited to the military.
Institutionalized overkill is well established among large
bureaucracies in every field—hospitals, universities, and
big tech companies all run into the same problem. That's
no great revelation, but it still feels good to say it out loud.

Whether it makes sense or not, whether it helps or not,
in large organizations standards have been established in
which projects are subjected to layers of assessment and
review that are considered useless by most of the people involved (including the reviewers themselves, truth be told)
but which everyone participates in anyway, largely because
there is a belief that there is nothing that they can do about
it. I used the passive voice and committed other grammatical travesties in the previous sentence on purpose to convey
the thoughtless, depersonalized beigeness of the situation.
I promise, I won't write like that anymore.

Because large organizations tend to err on the side of
overdoing it, project leaders feel compelled to spend large
quantities of time and money on Gordian knot–inspired
oversight processes that in no way increase the quality or
value of the product. This leads some to complain that such
projects could easily be fast, inexpensive, restrained, and

elegant if the review processes were only simplified and streamlined. Not to worry—FIRE is here to help, and the help begins by challenging the problem statement.

While streamlining the review process is a beautiful thing, formally and officially removing burdensome oversight from that process is not a prerequisite to implementing the ideas in this book. We can start to pursue speed, thrift, simplicity, and restraint long before streamlining the whole process. In fact, if we *start* with FIRE, under any policy or regulatory environment, we'll find it automatically reduces the amount of oversight a project is subjected to, and that it does so in an entirely aboveboard, appropriate way.

Excessive management oversight is primarily the result of lack of trust, and corporate trust tends to be eroded by three things: time, size, and problems. FIRE helps us reduce the impact of each of these erosive sources not by altering the nature of bureaucracy or radically redesigning the review process but by changing the structure of the project itself into something more conducive to trust. That's the part of the equation a project leader has the most influence on anyway, so it makes sense to start there.

First, let's talk about time. Even the most enlightened, most trustful, and least burdensome managers will want to be informed about changes to a project. As we saw previously, speed fosters stability and minimizes a project's exposure to change, which means a fast project has fewer changes to report to the higher-ups. If you are fortunate enough to work in an organization in which reviews are internally triggered by the events within the project itself, FIRE can help keep that to a minimum by reducing the amount of change.

Of course, in many organizations management reviews have *external* triggers. These organizations provide oversight not because the project needs review but because it is now Thursday or it is May or there's a full moon or some other equally valid reason. The longer our program lasts, the more often it will have to submit to things like quarterly or annual reviews. Obviously, the key to minimizing this source of oversight is to shorten the schedule.

If your organization cleverly decreed, "All projects shall submit to ye olde annual reviews" (whether they need them or not), you'll be subjected to this experience twice in a two-year program but will only have to do it once in a one-year program. Get your project done in less than a year, and you might skip that review entirely if you time it right. Whether these reviews are annual, monthly, weekly, or daily, each reduction in the schedule is also a reduction in the amount of time available to spend in a conference room going over said schedule. And this happens without having to change the official process.

If we use it right, speed can serve as a forcing function to reduce our project's obligation to perform ponderous reviews. For example, if we are scheduled to deliver a product next month, someone farther up in the hierarchy might nevertheless insist on delaying the delivery because the regularly scheduled Senior Technical Update Process Inquiry Delivery Meeting isn't held for another three months, and you really can't deliver until you've presented to the STUPID meeting, just like everyone else. In this situation, the absurdity of the suggestion will become immediately apparent, and you'll instantly, easily be granted a waiver. Ah, who am I kidding? You'll have a big fight on your hands, no question about it.

No, it won't be easy to convince the Defenders of the Status Quo that delivering on time makes more sense than delaying just so that the project fits some cookie-cutter timeline and satisfies the bureaucratic interests of incurious, inflexible corporate slugs who are more interested in eating doughnuts than actually reviewing your project anyway.

Oops, I think that was my outside voice. My point is, speed does not automatically get us a free pass out of the bland insanity of bureaucracyland. It does, however, improve our odds of success. It gives us a fighting chance, and frankly, that might be all we need.

If that third or fourth or seventeenth level of review is not going to add anything to the project, shortening the schedule and signing up to a short-term delivery date just might be the ticket to get off the not-so-merry-go-round. We may still be required to explain why delivering a product matters more than complying with the Process That Be, we may still have to fill out a waiver request form in triplicate, and we may still find ourselves engaged in existential debates ("What is the meaning of life? Why are we here? To execute a process? To review spreadsheets? Or to deliver super-awesome capability?"). But the alternative is to slow down in the name of compliance with corporate policies that are largely devoid of sense or value. I know which approach I prefer.

Let's move on to the question of size. Small teams of smart people have several advantages over larger organizational structures, not least of which is that small teams have less oversight. A team of ten thousand will automatically develop more layers of review and management than a team of three, partly due to limitations to span of control, partly due to the curiosity and initiative of the leaders, and partly due to the amount of money required to fund a large program. Bear in mind that "size" refers to several dimensions of the project, including the budget as well as the team. By reducing the amount of money expended on a project, we naturally reduce the amount of oversight it is subjected to. A multimillion-dollar project will simply attract more oversight attention than a less expensive one.

On the topic of multimillion-dollar projects, recall that a project leader's influence is inversely proportional to the size of the budget. This is partly a function of trust and risk, but ego and prestige play a role as well. Senior managers tend to pay less attention to inexpensive projects in part because the exposure to loss is small but also because such projects often do not merit the attention of someone of their esteemed status. Whether or not this is wise on their part is a question for another book. The point is that a project leader will have an easier time reducing oversight on a FIRE project than one with a huge budget.

Finally, even a fast, small project will attract oversight if it has a lot of problems. Fortunately, FIRE tends to reduce problems, in large part because of its emphasis on simplicity. A simpler technical architecture has fewer failure modes and interfaces to worry about. A simple organization has more streamlined and direct communication, which reduces confusion and ambiguity. If problems trigger oversight and FIRE prevents problems, we can conclude that FIRE helps reduce oversight.

I don't suggest trying to reduce oversight by talking people out of it or expecting the overseers to fundamentally change the way they view the world. That's not going to happen. Compliance-based organizations are notoriously resistant to logic and common sense. Rather than trying to change things beyond our control, we can use a judo technique (or maybe it's a Jedi mind trick) to focus on the pieces of the puzzle we can most directly influence and to present a smaller target to the forces of oversight.

Oversight and management review activities will never go away entirely, and that's all right. These things have value and can occasionally be helpful, both to the project and the overall organization, as long as we keep them in check. One way to minimize bureaucratic excess is to reduce the project's time, size, and problems. One such tool for cutting this particular Gordian knot is called the one-page project manager.

The One-Page Project Manager

A gentleman by the name of Clark Campbell developed a little thing he called the one-page project manager (OPPM), and in 2006 he published a book by the same name. The basic idea is that everything you need to know in order to manage a project can be presented on a single sheet of paper. It's an intriguing proposal.

Is the OPPM perfect? Of course not. Is it a good fit for your project? I have no idea. Are there instances where it would be useful or even superior to longer, more complex alternatives? Absolutely.

I am not saying you should definitely use the OPPM, nor am I particularly interested in testing and validating Campbell's claim that his approach can be used for "any project—no matter how big or complicated." I am content to simply observe that such a thing exists and to offer it for your consideration.

The deeper point is that *things like this exist*. The OPPM

is a single data point, an exemplar of the alternatives available to us when we seek to follow Alexander the Great's example and apply simplicity to complex problems. While this particular tool may or may not be relevant to your specific situation, it shows that the complexity and bulkiness of status quo management tools need not be inevitable. Simpler options are out there. If you haven't done so already, you may want to check a few of them out. Even if you decide not to use any of them, it might be informative and useful to know how they work.

Endless Gantt charts and multi-gigabyte Microsoft Project files contain important information, to be sure. They capture details about the project's past, present, and future, about the interrelationships between various elements. But these programmatic artifacts imply a metamessage, and that not-so-subtle message goes something like this: *We have a very complex project. Therefore I must be very smart and must be working very hard.*

If you're on the receiving end of this message, don't be fooled; if you are the one sending the message, don't fool yourself. Awkward though it may be to admit, it's possible that the mountainous stack of documents and charts we created only represents effort, not skill. Throwing more and more information into a pile without regard to its value, without performing rigorous and thoughtful analysis, probably indicates lazy thinking, not professional competence. All the data in the world is worthless if it doesn't actually mean something, and it only means something if we can understand it.

To be fair, just as the big, complex approach can fail to communicate effectively, an OPPM could provide a dangerously oversimplified representation of the program, failing to bring certain trends, risks, or opportunities to our attention. Clearly, lazy thinking provides bad results, whether said laziness is expressed as unfiltered complexity or incomplete simplicity. I've found the former to be more common than the latter, but your individual results may vary.

Whether we're using the OPPM or a longer, more traditional tool, we need to exert a certain amount of thoughtful effort. To assess the merits of these two approaches, I recommend comparing the best versions of both, not the worst. Imagine you are handed a clear, comprehensive set of traditional program management artifacts—the best possible stack of charts, spreadsheets, schedules, and everything. Presumably these would reside in a set of large binders, in long meetings, in a collection of computer files, or in all of the above.

Now, imagine being handed a well-executed one-pager. Which would you prefer? Which would be more useful, helpful, and informative? In my opinion, the good OPPM comes out looking rather appealing, even when compared to the best-case version of the longer alternative.

I would also suggest that it is easier to use the traditional tools badly, which is an important thing to keep in mind. I'm less impressed with a powerful tool if it tends to nudge us in unproductive directions. The fact is, the expansive nature of most project management tools reinforces the idea that more information is better, which is why so many schedules and spreadsheets go on as long as they do.

With many traditional program management tools, the bias toward adding things is baked into the tool's structure, and there are precious few limits on the number of fields, columns, rows, sheets, or pages we can create. As we're about to see, information overload reduces decision quality, and this is precisely the sort of error Campbell's OPPM aims to prevent. The whole structure of the one-pager is oriented toward providing only the critical, important information. This restrained approach helps keep us focused on the necessary and undistracted by the extraneous.

During the Faster, Better, Cheaper era, NASA's hugely successful Near Earth Asteroid Rendezvous (NEAR) mission used an approach that sounds a lot like the OPPM. Recall, NEAR Shoemaker engineers gave three-minute reports and used a simple twelve-line schedule to manage the project. Their mission predates Campbell's work and offers an independent data point supporting the idea that a restrained approach can be meaningful and productive.

Maybe the one-page project manager isn't right for you. Perhaps you'd be better off with a two-pager or even a three-pager. And sure, some projects really, really need a gazillion-page project manager.

No, not really. Nobody needs a gazillion-pager. And yet, that's what most of us use, isn't it? All the more reason to look at the OPPM.

While endless schedule files and bottomless documents are fine examples of modern Gordian knottiness, the most beknotted realm of corporate practice is surely the Power-Point presentation, which is the topic of our next segment.

Let's All Smoke Marijuana!

Here's an idea: the next time you are about to give a big presentation to a group of senior leaders, go out and buy some marijuana from your friendly neighborhood drug dealer. Before you begin speaking, pass a couple of joints around the conference room. Once all are sufficiently baked, ask them to pay attention to your charts and to make good decisions based on the information you present. Let me know how that works out for you.

While I must admit I have never actually performed that experiment, I have a pretty good idea what the results would be. I'm told marijuana tends to impair, not improve, judgment. So maybe this wouldn't be such a good idea after all.

You know what would be just as crazy? Giving a Power Point presentation using the typical template, with its endless stream of bullet points in tiny font. And I literally mean *just as crazy*, because a 2005 study at King's College London by psychiatrist Glenn Wilson showed that information overload impairs concentration and degrades decision quality as much as smoking weed does. In fact, information overload was equivalent to a loss of ten IQ points, while lighting up a doobie drops a person's IQ by approximately five points. So maybe the typical approach to PowerPoint is even crazier than going for a dance with Mary Jane.

Yet the average PowerPoint presentation contains precisely 1.21 gigawatts of information, putting audience members into an information overload situation almost immediately. Dense charts filled with cheap clip art and jumbled diagrams are treated like some sort of perverse best practice, while the phrase "I know you can't read this chart" is accepted as a reasonable statement rather than a cause for revolt. Don't get me started on the ubiquitous logos and slogans we plaster around the corners and edges of. Every. Single. Chart.

No need to prolong my rant. I'm sure you are either already painfully aware of the situation, in which case you don't need me to tell you how bad most corporate communication is, or you work in a place where this does not occur, in which case you can safely skip to the next section. The same goes for anyone who has read Garr Reynolds's fantastic book *Presentation Zen*, which points out that "no one can do a good presentation with slide after slide of bullet points," among other important insights.

Applying FIRE to a PowerPoint deck means placing a premium on clarity, brevity, and restraint to ensure we communicate effectively. The guiding heuristic is that each chart should contain between half an idea and one idea, no more. This generally translates into relatively few words per chart, better use of imagery, and simpler diagrams.

When a chart presents two or more ideas, it is almost a guarantee that the speaker will be talking about one idea while the audience's attention is focused on something else. When a chart contains a dozen different topics, we might as well just pass the dutchie on the left-hand side.

By limiting each chart's content to a single idea (or less!), we increase the odds of aligning the speaker's words, the visual content, and the audience's attention. That is important, because misalignment between words, content, and attention is a leading cause of the munchies.

This approach likely requires a deviation from the standard template, particularly if the template includes the dreaded quad chart. For those fortunate readers who are not familiar with the abomination known as a quad chart, it is what it sounds like: a single chart, divided into four quadrants, each of which is filled to overflowing with different information about the project being presented. One section might be a project description, while another might show the budget; a third might present the schedule in excruciatingly small print ("I'm sorry, I know nobody can read this . . ."). The fourth section is often a diagram of some sort, or perhaps a list of current problems, issues, and/or accomplishments. Why anyone thinks we need to see all of that information on a screen at one time is a mystery beyond my comprehension, particularly in light of research that indicates mental multitasking leads to worse decisions.* A quad chart design might be useful as a reference sheet when printed and carried by hand, but there is no excuse for projecting it onto a screen before a conference room full of people.

Interestingly, when a quad is displayed, the Very Important Person on the receiving end of the presentation typically holds up a hand in the classic traffic-cop pose and asks for a moment of silence in order to gain orientation and begin absorbing the information on the screen. This can be a very long moment indeed. Of course, maybe that person is just feeling particularly mellow and needs a minute. As those King's College researchers showed, sometimes it can be hard to tell the difference between information overload and feeling groovy.

How should we proceed if the mandated format insists we produce a quad chart or a similarly dense, convoluted, ineffective presentation? At the very least, we can break it up into four individual charts. Go ahead. It's all right. Tell them I said you have my permission. If you need to, you can use the excuse that your eyes aren't good enough to see it, so you had to make the thing larger. Alternatively, you could say you want to draw the audience's attention to some finer details that would be obscured in the standard quad format. Both explanations are honest; nobody's eyes

---

* See "Cognitive Control in Media Multitaskers," *Proceedings of the National Academy of Sciences*, September 2009.

are that good, and you presumably do want to make sure your audience's concentration is not affected. That's why you didn't bring any weed today.

One reasonable accommodation might be to display the quad for the briefest of moments in a sign of good faith and compliance with the expectations of corporate normalcy. Then click to the next chart, which shows a zoomed-in look at one quarter of the quad. Want to get really crazy? One more click could bring you to a new chart displaying an even deeper zoom, highlighting the one thing you want to make really clear. In this way we can show that we are good corporate citizens but also clear communicators.

Spreading information out this way actually saves time in the presentation by preventing anyone (including the speaker) from getting lost or distracted. If we do it well, the end result will be increased clarity and understanding. Anyone who complains about that outcome clearly has a different agenda, in which case we've got bigger problems to worry about.

My more mathematically inclined readers have by now figured out that this approach would increase the number of charts in our presentation by at least a factor of four. Yes. Yes, it will. And that's okay.

While FIRE insists on tight limits to document page counts (more on that shortly), these limits are expressed differently when we are talking about a presentation. See, the limited resource at hand is almost always time. Rather than limiting the number of charts a speaker can use, we should establish a limit on the time the speaker can spend. If the speaker can get through forty charts in five minutes, and does so in a way that communicates clearly, he or she should be allowed to do so. In fact, we should insist on it.

For some of us this will require a proactive stance. I've lost track of the number of times I've heard the phrase "You can only use one chart when you brief Mr. Smith," as if PowerPoint charts were a limited resource requiring careful conservation measures.

If you ever find yourself in that unfortunate situation, consider taking this course of action:

1. Ask how much time is available.
2. Promise to say your piece within the allocated time.
3. Explain that for the sake of clarity and time you will use more than one chart. This explanatory step is optional, and in some cases revealing your plans in advance may be inadvisable.
4. Promise again to stay within the time limit.
5. Put no more than one idea into each chart. Use as many charts as you need to communicate in a clear and focused way.
6. Finish on time. This step is not optional.

For the environmentally conscious among us who may be concerned about the amount of paper required to print all these extra charts, fear not! These charts can easily be printed two or even six per page, without any loss of legibility, because unlike the standard stack of twelve-point bullets used in a quad chart, your charts will still be readable when compressed and printed into a three-by-two matrix.

The principle here is that time is a precious commodity, while charts are cheap. It costs us virtually nothing to turn one chart into four or even ten. It costs a lot indeed to waste an hour failing to communicate clearly.

This brings us to the topic of documents. Unlike a

presentation, a document's page count correlates closely with the amount of time required to digest the material because information density per page is much less variable than information density per slide. We can put one or two words on a slide, leave it on the screen for a few seconds, and then quickly move on to the next slide. The same approach is less effective in a document.

Page count matters because page count is a proxy for time. Since the FIRE approach places a premium on speed (i.e., efficient use of time), it encourages us to keep our documents short and focused. The result not only saves the reader's time but also saves time in reviewing, coordinating, and correcting the document. But the real benefit is that a short document is less likely to obscure its own message. Yes, this approach saves time, and that's important. It also communicates more effectively, which is even more important.

In most projects, there is actually no such thing as *a* document. Instead, we have dozens, hundreds, or even thousands of documents, which introduces a whole new set of challenges.

The key is to winnow down that stack to an absolute minimum and refuse to tolerate the presence of valueless documents that are produced only to satisfy an obscure checklist but have no relationship to the project's actual execution. This accumulation is sometimes referred to as dusty binder syndrome; the documents sit on shelves, unread, forming a sad memorial to wasted effort.

FIRE also encourages minimizing duplication among documents. While the same data is presented in multiple reports, the project team faces the unenviable task of making sure each document is up-to-date and consistent with all the others. This is not only unnecessary, unproductive effort (our "lean manufacturing" friends call it waste) but also a potential source of much confusion, angst, frustration, embarrassment, and otherwise misaligned activity.

Ideally, each piece of important information about the project should occur once in a single document. It should be sufficient for other documents to refer to the master document rather than restate that which has been already explained. For example, I once came across the following line in a planning document: "As explained in Section 3.2.1, the contract for PROJECT X has not been awarded yet. Once the contract for PROJECT X is awarded, the contractor for PROJECT X will begin working on PROJECT X."

I promise, the only thing I changed in those sentences was the project's name, which I obscured to protect the guilty. What we see here is a restating of something already explained earlier in the document, followed by a statement of the obvious, and no fewer than four references to the project's name. The whole document went on like that, so it should come as no surprise that the first twenty-six pages of the hundred-plus-page document were a preamble to the actual topic. Surely we can do better than that.

Of course, sometimes it happens that we are handed a blank template that is 327 pages long before we add any content. In such a situation, we are not being set up for success, but neither is doom inevitable.

There is no secret to fixing this situation, no shockingly original approach that will blow your socks off. What FIRE suggests is to trim the heck out of the template. Are some portions of it irrelevant to your project? Yes. Definitely. Absolutely. You can safely ignore them. Delete them. Mark them "n/a" and don't look back.

By all means, have a conversation about this with whoever gave you the template and/or whoever plans to receive the finished product. Explain your decision and make sure you don't inadvertently leave out some critical piece of information. There's no need to do this in the blind. But there is also no need to blindly accept every template as holy writ. In ninety-nine cases out of a hundred, we can make changes to the template without inadvertently triggering the end of the world. Well, when I put it that way, it's more like a hundred cases out of a hundred.

This approach shows initiative and thought. It is efficient and communicates clearly. It also puts the onus on the gatekeepers and status quo defenders to explain why they need all that clutter in the first place.

And to avoid any confusion, let me state for the record that I don't recommend bringing a bunch of joints to your next presentation. Stay in school, kids. Don't do drugs.

Measurements and Metrics

Some Gordian knots manage to obscure our understanding of the situation without appearing to be complex. These misdirected knots point us in the wrong direction and introduce confusion despite their seeming simplicity. Such is the case with certain measurement regimes.

Atul Gawande is a surgeon, journalist, and best-selling author. He was named a MacArthur Fellow in 2006, an honor reserved for an extremely elite group known colloquially as "geniuses." In his second book, *Better*, Gawande suggests that someone who wants to improve her performance in any field of activity "should be a scientist in this world. In the simplest terms, this means one should count something."

It's good advice, maybe even genius-level advice, because of its simplicity and practicality, and I heartily recommend following it. But as we commit to counting something, it's also wise to make sure we think clearly about the thing we're counting.

For example, I know a guy who, at age forty, has a thirty-one-inch waist, runs a mile and a half in less than nine minutes and thirty seconds, and regularly scores a perfect 100 on his annual military fitness test. However, at five foot eleven and 180 pounds, his body mass index (BMI) is 25.1, which technically puts him in the overweight category. I think we'd all love to be overweight like him.

Another buddy showed me his latest annual perfor-mance review and laughingly pointed out that it didn't say much of anything. Sure, there were lots of nice words and impressive-sounding statistics, and the general tone was positive, but this report completely failed to address his most noted accomplishments of the past year. Instead, it focused on the trivial and easily measured.

I've certainly found that to be the case in my career. In any given year, my most important achievements and con-tributions to my unit's mission—the mentoring sessions with a young officer, the small decisions that prevented large problems down the road—are nowhere to be found in my official performance assessment. Instead, what end up on my record are the measurable, obvious activities that sound important but really aren't. A strictly informal and unscientific survey of my colleagues suggests my situation is not unique. Our reports count things, but not the things that count.

Both BMI calculations and quantified performance re-views have their place and can be useful, accurate tools in some circumstances. Nevertheless, they have severe limits, and the aforementioned examples show the danger of counting things that are easy to count but do not provide much insight. Beware convenient metrics.

My athletic friend is trim and muscular. He does not need to lose weight, even though his BMI score indicates otherwise. To be fair, the BMI literature is quite explicit that it does not apply to highly athletic people, but all too often we overlook that disclaimer and end up misinterpreting the data.

This is what happened to a 2013 Pentagon report that scientifically claimed that precisely "51.2% of service members are overweight," based solely on BMI calculations. Interestingly, that report correctly discounted the calculation, explaining that BMI "does not account for body muscle mass which may contribute to the high rate of overweight service members." This begs the question of why the BMI would be mentioned in the first place if its results are so misleading and irrelevant when applied to an athletic population like the military. It makes me wonder why a different measurement wasn't used. Unfortunately the disclaimer did not prevent several media outlets from publishing headlines suggesting that the majority of US armed forces personnel are pudgy.

Similarly, despite the vapid wording of my other buddy's performance report, he did some fantastic things last year. You just can't tell what they were by looking at his performance review. If these were isolated, rare instances, we could write them off as anomalies. Sadly, they are all too common.

Gawande's advice about the importance and value of counting things is correct. We should indeed live as scientists in this world. We should count things, track trends, analyze statistics, and do other interesting things with the numbers we collect. But along the way we should also make sure our counting conveys meaning. That way, when we meet a sleek athlete with a BMI score greater than 25, we won't prescribe an unnecessary weight-loss regimen. And if a spreadsheet reveals a whole battalion of such troops, we won't incorrectly call them fat.

If we want to use the FIRE approach scientifically, what should we count? What should we measure? Well, if the old chestnut about getting what we reward is true, then we should probably measure what we want so we'll know whether to reward it or not. Since FIRE suggests that speed, thrift, simplicity, and self-control correlate with excellent outcomes, let's begin our measurement discussion there.

We'll need to decide on units of measurement, and it is here we encounter the first challenge. Speed and thrift are relatively easy to measure, because we can talk about units of time and money, but what units do we use to count elegance? What are the units of restraint?

For that matter, even measuring time and money can be a bit more complicated than it sounds. Should we count calendar days or man-hours? When do we start the clock, and when do we stop it? Do we track projections of future expenditures or only count dollars that have actually been spent? Should we subtract dollars saved from dollars spent? And how much granularity do we need—should we track expenses to the penny on a daily basis? Or might the cost of such a tracking mechanism exceed any savings it might convey?

Okay, hold on. Before we get all wrapped around the axle, let's remind ourselves why we're doing this. As tempting as it might be to launch a huge, expensive, complex, time-consuming measurement initiative, such an approach is counterproductive if we're trying to be fast, inexpensive, restrained, and elegant, right? Maybe we can find a simpler way to proceed.

I wish I could provide a comprehensive set of universal FIRE metrics that would apply to every project, a virtual yardstick or measuring cup everyone could use to easily assess a project. I can't, because FIRE can be applied to everything from dishwashers to spaceships. This limits how specific we can get. Plus, like apples in the fall, your particular statistics will mean more if you pick them yourself.

My suggestion, therefore, is to create your own simple set of indicators, one that will shine a light on the levels of speed, thrift, simplicity, and restraint in your project. You almost certainly do not need a hundred such measurements—probably three or four is the right number. Eight might be tolerable if it's two for each piece of FIRE, but that is really pushing the limit. Any more than that is overkill.

While I can't prescribe a specific set of measurements for everyone to collect on every project, I can offer a few guidelines for how to count with FIRE.

1. Count something. It is truly surprising how often projects fail to do this part. Many team members have no idea how much time or money they're spending, let alone how much complexity they are dealing with or how much the project has grown. This is particularly acute on big projects with large teams, in which such programmatic details can become ignored or

obscured in the general ebb and flow of busyness. So count page numbers. Count team size. Count the duration, frequency, and size of meetings. Count lines of code. Count gross vehicle weight. Along the way, keep in mind that increasing those numbers does not always represent progress.

2. Do it publicly. Data about your project's progress should be hard to miss, not hard to find, so make sure the whole team is able to put eyeballs on it. Better yet, make sure each team member knows how he or she contributes to the figures, and how each can help bring the numbers down. Naturally, this is much easier if your team is small—as it should be.

3. Track trends, not just static figures. Where we are at the moment matters less than where we're heading. Past trends often (but not always!) indicate where we are heading in the future, but even when a trend is not predictive it might show whether we've made progress or not. It might also reveal causal relationships, such as a decrease in complexity every time the boss goes on vacation. That observation can help shape future activities.

4. Focus on critical figures. The program management discipline is full of clever-sounding approaches to measurement, with names that beg to be introduced to the edge of Alexander the Great's sword, such as MTBCFMARS or EVMBCWPTD. Don't fall for it. Numbers and figures can be hypnotic, but these long lists of obscure and esoteric measurements tend to point to minor nuance rather than key lever points. It is important to make sure the things we're counting really count. I wish I could say that goes without

saying, but I've been in this business long enough to know otherwise.

5. Focus on meaning more than precision. Use your measurements to complement qualitative insights, not do away with them. A gut impression of complexity is often just as useful as a scientific, statistically rigorous measurement, and we generally notice complexity has increased long before we can quantify it. This doesn't let us off the hook for counting things; it just means we might know the answer even before the counting is complete.

Now, gut impressions can be wrong and nobody's intuition is reliable all the time, but the same caveat applies to concrete measurements. The thing is, we may talk about emotions coming from the heart or instinct from the gut, but they actually come from the same brain as our rational analyses. We all possess a capacity for subconscious information processing that sometimes leads us to good decisions we can't explain. Keep that in mind as you do your counting.

Gawande's advice is right on. As scientists in the world, we should count something. We should also make sure the counting counts. When we choose to use a measurement with a narrow range of relevance like the BMI, we need to be careful with our conclusions.

Let's also make sure our measurements do not become ends unto themselves. As scientists, we count things to help us understand the world, to reveal patterns and relationships, to identify areas where performance is excellent or improvement is needed. As project managers and leaders, we count things to shape behavior—our own and that of our teammates. We should emphatically avoid counting things just for the sake of counting, or to populate a spreadsheet that creates a graph that goes into a report that nobody reads or needs.

The best measurement regimens are themselves expressions of the FIRE approach. They are developed and updated in the natural course of events, with minimal investment of time and money. They answer questions we actually ask, or cause us to ask questions whose answers matter. They are tightly correlated with performance, and are simple to understand and apply. They are clear, coherent, and relevant to the population being counted. And there are only a handful of them. Identifying that small handful requires thoughtful effort and experimentation, unlike the intellectually lazy approach that simply throws more and more figures into a big pile of files because the people involved can't decide which ones matter.

If you are not counting anything yet, it is time to start. If you already have an intensive, costly measurement program, take a closer look and see if there are opportunities to simplify, streamline, and reduce it to its essentials. And if you're calculating someone's BMI, don't overlook the limitations of that particular index, because if you call my friend fat, he just might challenge you to a race.

From misleading measurement programs and convoluted bureaucracies to endless PowerPoint presentations and reports, Gordian knots take many forms. As Alexander the Great showed us, such complexities are best overcome by the judicious application of simplicity. Chapter 7 takes a look at the relationship between simplicity and complexity and offers a road map to help us avoid complexity-related pitfalls.

Simplicity and Complexity

Imagine being challenged to design a toy hovercraft that a child can build. Imagine further that the instructions for building this toy must fit on a single sheet of paper. Also, the instructions should teach a little science lesson while you're at it, still without exceeding that one-page limit. And it should be fun. One last thing: the hovercraft needs to be made out of ordinary household objects, preferably trash, so a kid can assemble it without having to make a trip to the store or spend any money at all. Sounds impossible, I know, but you can see what a solution to that challenge looks like at Howtoons.com.

The geniuses who run that website provide directions on how to make a toy hovercraft out of three parts: a CD, a balloon, and a nozzle from a soap bottle. Just glue the nozzle over the hole in the middle of the CD, attach the inflated balloon to the nozzle, and, voilà—you have a functioning hovercraft. Move the nozzle into the open position, and as the balloon deflates it will create a cushion of air beneath the CD that lifts the craft up from your work surface. Several other websites offer similar designs, and it's not clear who came up with the idea in the first place, but Howtoons presents the whole concept in a single page.

What does this project teach? Well, the most obvious lesson is about friction and inertia. Want to experience Isaac Newton's first law of motion? Just nudge the hovercraft while it's sitting directly on a table, then again when the nozzle is open and the balloon is venting. In hover mode, that little toy will glide forever in response to a slight nudge. At rest, it barely flinches. Newton would be proud.

The hovercraft also teaches something about air pressure as we watch the balloon deflate. It may even teach a subtle lesson about gravity, since the craft only lifts a fraction of an inch off the table.

But there's an even more important—and subtler—lesson at work here: simplicity, thrift, speed, and restraint are possible. Yes, the hovercraft teaches FIRE. See, the seemingly impossible challenge of creating do-it-yourself instructions for an educational, super-low-cost toy hovercraft on one piece of paper is actually possible.

This little toy, which I personally enjoyed making and playing with, exemplifies all the FIRE principles, beginning with a tight focus on a narrow set of requirements. Consider this: the object is to make a hovercraft, so the device must ride on a cushion of air. That is pretty much the only requirement. It does not have to be steerable. It does not have to haul a heavy load. It doesn't need a television marketing campaign and its own line of breakfast cereal. In order to be a hovercraft, it simply has to hover.

They say good things come in threes, and there are actually two more requirements to consider. The object is also a toy, so the second requirement is that it has to be fun—and it is. Don't take my word for it. Go ahead and make one of your own and see how much fun it is. It won't take much time or money. In fact, it might not cost you anything at all. Because I already had an old CD, an empty soap bottle, and some glue, the only thing it cost me was $1.50 for a bag of balloons. And I literally spent more time looking for my hot glue gun than actually assembling the hovercraft. The ease and speed of assembly definitely contributed to the fun, because I didn't have to sweat over tiny pieces or wait a long time. So, it was fun to make *and* fun to play with.

Finally, the hovercraft is an *educational* toy, so the final requirement is that it needs to teach something. We've already addressed that.

So much for the three functional requirements (hover, be fun, teach). We might want to consider the programmatic requirements, just for kicks. This toy had a requirement to be inexpensive and easy to build in a short amount of time with few moving parts. Among other things, these constraints nudged the design in the direction of using found materials.

The military refers to this approach as commercial off-the-shelf, or COTS. I'm pretty sure the commercial world just calls it reuse. Whatever the term, the COTS approach basically involves repurposing existing components and systems into new applications. When done well, this approach can help contain the cost, complexity, and time associated with building a new product. When done badly, it can be a disaster, of course. The secret to doing it badly is to insist on extensive modifications to the existing product rather than using it as is (aka off-the-shelf). In our hovercraft example, that might involve buying a special drill so we can expand the size of the hole in the middle of the CD or, worse yet, trying to mold the CD into a slightly concave shape in the name of improved aerodynamics.

As it turns out, extensively modifying COTS is usually a terrible idea. In the case of our hovercraft, an old CD could not be better suited for our needs if it was custom-made to our exact specifications. It is lightweight, rigid, strong, and—if we arrange it label side down—even has a shiny, futuristically silver appearance that is awesome.

The hole in the middle is a perfect size—not too big, not too small. The fact that a CD is circular means our air cushion is evenly distributed across the entire surface. If a team of PhD engineers were to sit down and design an ideal hovercraft platform, it would look exactly like a CD. Unless, of course, they overvalued complexity and viewed a large budget as a sign of prestige, in which case it would probably have flying buttresses, spoilers, and wings. But that would be wrong.

The same goes for the soap bottle nozzle. It is virtually unbreakable and fits perfectly over the hole in the CD, and when it is in the closed position it is completely airtight. It easily snaps open, and as an added bonus, it's free. Sure, you may have to wait until that bottle of soap is empty, but speaking as a parent, maybe this is an opportunity to motivate the kids to wash the dishes. Speaking as an *experienced* parent, you may want to monitor how much soap the munchkins use. Speaking as a systems engineer and program manager, using up all the soap on one dinner's worth of dishes just so they can get to the nozzle is what we call an unintended consequence of a misaligned incentive.

And then there is the craft's power source—the balloon. It is cheap, reusable, and replaceable. When it breaks or loses its elasticity, it can be discarded and a new balloon put in place. While we're talking about disposal, let me mention that both the old CD and the soap nozzle are items I was going to throw away. This means their cost to me is zero and their cost to the planet is actually negative, at least temporarily, because they were rescued from entering the refuse pipeline and ending up in a landfill.

This particular toy might not provide years and years of fun, but the return on investment is quite large because the investment itself is so small. That is an important calculation to make. So if you are looking for an enjoyable way to spend a little time playing and learning with your kids, this little hovercraft more than fits the bill. Build a couple of them, add some stickers, and have races if you want to extend the fun.

In a similar fashion, not every technology development project has to be one for the ages. Rather than building or buying a jet, satellite, or full-size hovercraft that will last for decades and provide dozens of different capabilities, we might be better off building or buying a simple, stripped-down, good-enough object that does one or two things really, really well. Google's stripped-down Chromebook laptop, which provides all its functions via web applications, comes to mind. Some of us need more function than the Chromebook provides, but few of us need all the capabilities provided by a typical laptop.

Unlike the little toy hovercraft, we can't build every system out of 66 percent trash. And to be sure, not every system should be disposable. But it is a bit silly to expect any approach to be applicable to every system and every need. On that note, not every system should be expected to last for fifty years. This is no great insight, of course. The point is simply that we can—and should—be open to simple, scaled-down solutions. They may be exactly what we need.

The Simplicity Cycle

The homemade hovercraft story demonstrates that simplicity can be a valuable attribute for a finished product. What we haven't seen yet is how difficult it is to achieve and maintain such an admirable degree of simplicity. See, whether you're designing a new piece of software, printing a gizmo on your 3-D printer, or putting together charts for a presentation, creeping complexity always tries to eat your lunch, waste your time, and generally make things difficult for you and the people around you. The worst part is, so much of this complexity is self-inflicted.

Actually, strike that. The worst part is it's *deliberately* self-inflicted. Not only do we make things more complicated than necessary, we do it on purpose. Why does this happen? It happens because we often think a high level of complexity is both inevitable and desirable. The truth is, it's neither.

At the root of this problem is a tendency to equate complexity with sophistication. That's an understandable belief; up to a certain point, more complexity does mean a better product. But things head south when we go beyond that "certain point." It's terribly easy to cross the line, particularly if we're not looking for it. That's where the simplicity cycle comes in.

The primary insight conveyed by the simplicity cycle is that complexity and goodness are not always directly proportional. That is, making something more complicated isn't the same as making it better. It's one of those design principles that sounds obvious when we say it out loud, but in practice it is often ignored. Why do we ignore such an obvious concept? We've actually got a pretty good excuse for this illogical behavior. People tend to associate complexity with superiority because of our experience in the early stages of a design.

You see, as a piece of technology develops from a rudimentary model to a more advanced one, it tends to accumulate new parts, features, and components. Advanced (i.e., better) models tend to do more, not less. The same is true for books, articles, and PowerPoint presentations; adding stuff makes them more interesting, more informative, and more useful. The catch is, this relationship does not continue indefinitely. The design behaviors that initially improve the product (i.e., adding stuff) eventually become counterproductive (i.e., adding too much stuff). The result is a mess.

Figure 7.1 illustrates this dynamic using an arrow that moves from the lower left corner to the middle of the diagram, and then splits into two branches.

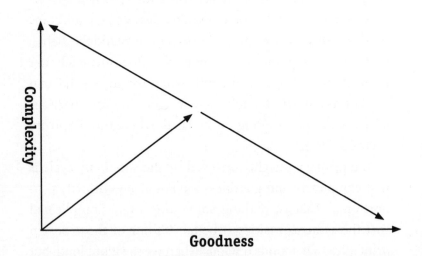

FIGURE 7.1. THE SIMPLICITY CYCLE

The arrow from the bottom left corner to the middle of the diagram describes the way a design simultaneously becomes more complex *and* better. This typically happens in the early stages of the design. The middle of the diagram is where our design hits a critical mass of complexity and everything changes.

From that point, continuing to move up and to the right is impossible. Once we reach the center point, adding complexity no longer makes the design better. Instead, adding complexity moves the design up and to the left, meaning the system gets more complicated and *worse*. The alternative is to reduce complexity, which moves the design down and to the right, making the design *simpler and better*. Clearly, down and right is the best way to go. Unfortunately, up and left is much more common because that's the direction our design momentum carries us.

The key is to avoid being lulled into inattention by the inertia of our early progress. As a design matures, we must focus on making the thing *better* and not be satisfied with merely making it *more complex*. There's a difference.

The other key is to know when to stop adding stuff and start removing stuff. That applies whether you're writing code, building an organization, creating a presentation, or designing a spaceship.

Having identified the need to stop making things more complicated, the really hard work begins: making things simpler. As Steve Jobs famously explained, "Focusing is about saying no. And the result of that focus is going to be some really great products where the total is much greater than the sum of the parts."

Saying no is hugely important. Sometimes we even have to say no to things that previously got a yes, taking things that originally looked like good ideas out of a design. That is exactly what's happening as we move from the middle of the chart to the lower right corner.

The simplicity cycle concept posits that complexity is ultimately a sign of an immature design, not a sophisticated one. So when you hear people brag about how very, very complicated their design is, feel free to shake your head and mutter, "I have a very bad feeling about this."

Occasionally, someone will suggest that this concept is fine if we want to build a simple system but that it doesn't work if we want to build a complex system. The word choice is particularly revealing: "we *want* to build . . ." All too often, people view high levels of complexity as admirable. That's unfortunate and unnecessary.

Yes, there's a certain amount of inevitable complexity for any given product. Any Internet-related object that doesn't play well with others is going to lose points, so for reasons of interconnectedness alone today's systems will be more complex than comparable stuff from earlier eras. But that just means that the floor of complexity is higher than it used to be, not that designers should tolerate *unnecessary* complexity.

Once we accept the idea that simplicity is both desirable and possible, we can begin taking steps to reduce the complexity of our organizations, processes, and technologies. Toward that end, the TRIZ community (see chapter 2) offers an interesting and powerful technique called trimming. It's illustrated in figure 7.2.

Basically, the idea is to remove something from your design and try to make it work with the remaining pieces. However, there's a bit more nuance to it than that. For example, the "Does system work?" block may require making

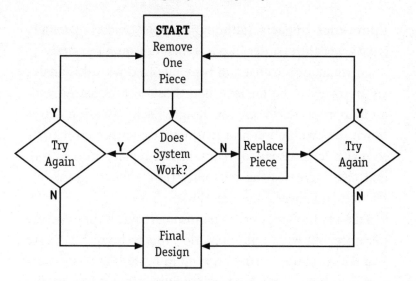

FIGURE 7.2. A TRIMMING FLOWCHART

some changes to the remaining design elements in order to get to a *yes* answer. As long as the tweaks and modifications don't involve adding more features, parts, or functions, they are probably consistent with the intent of this practice. It really is as simple as that.

Trimming is a simple little practice, but not necessarily easy. It might take more than a little imagination and cleverness to figure out how to accomplish the mission in the absence of a particular component, particularly after the third or fourth time through the loop. At first glance, each and every part in your design may seem essential. But with a little experimentation and imagination, I think you'll find you can cut many, many pieces that previously seemed essential.

Bear in mind that you'll want to do several tests and trials to make sure the thing *really* works after each deletion. It's important to watch out for unintended consequences and third-order impacts (although simple objects generally have fewer third-order impacts than do complex ones).

Fortunately, the cost and time involved with this analysis are likely to be far less than those of proceeding with an inappropriately complex design. Each reduction drives down the production and maintenance costs (fewer parts to make, fewer parts to maintain and replace, and so on), and also increases the reliability (fewer parts means less friction and fewer failure modes).

Like any tool, mastery of trimming requires time and experience, but with a little practice, this technique can take you far. As you experiment, keep in mind that some parts and functions can't be permanently removed from the design without introducing a critical failure. Those are the essential pieces. Most of the time, the number of essential components is much smaller than it appears at first glance.

We set the stage for our own frustration when simplicity is not a design goal and when simplification is not part of our design discipline. All too often we aim for complexity and hit it—then get surprised when it hits us back. The good news is there's something we can do about it. Tools like the simplicity cycle and practices like trimming are good places to start. Another tool to consider is a little something I call stormdraining.

Stormdraining

Who doesn't love a good brainstorming session? Inhibitions are low, judgment is suspended, and a good time is had by all. Plus, there are usually doughnuts.

Set aside for a moment any critiques of brainstorming itself, any objections that it is neither efficient nor effective, or that studies show it produces suboptimal results. The fact is that brainstorming is a well-established practice that will likely continue to be used in conference rooms around the world for the foreseeable future. And that's all right.

Brainstorming is clearly a pretty good way to produce lot of ideas, if you're into that sort of thing. But if we stop there, we can seriously miss the point. Suspending judgment is good as long as it isn't a permanent condition. At some point, we need to reengage our critical thinking skills and get rid of all the stupid ideas we created so proudly.

It is entirely possible we've done a terrible thing to our brains by participating in so many fun, doughnut-filled brainstorming sessions. Using classical conditioning, we may have inadvertently trained ourselves and our teams to associate additive activities like brainstorming with both physical and psychological rewards. It feels good. We want to do more of it, even outside an official brainstorming activity. And undoing it makes us feel uncomfortable, maybe even sad and doughnut-deprived.

This creates a tendency to continue adding things—to our designs, organizations, processes, and presentations—long after such additions have stopped being useful. The result is thoughtlessly bloated structures and excessive feature sets.

To counter this tendency we need to create a parallel, complementary practice that rewards and encourages the opposite of brainstorming. We need a way to sort the wheat from the chaff and rescue the baby from the bathwater.

Let's refer to this activity as stormdraining. If a brainstorm produces a lot of ideas, a stormdrain provides a mechanism for preventing stagnant pools of idea water from turning into breeding grounds for mental mosquitoes and protects us from whatever organizational viruses those mosquitoes might carry.

To be fair, brainstorming in actual practice is generally followed by a phase of binning, sorting, sifting, and deleting. But we usually do this immediately after a brainstorming session, when we're feeling a bit tired; better to do it when we're fresh and energetic. Besides, this behavior requires a substantial shift in perspective—so much so that it should be given a cool name all its own and considered separately from brainstorming.

Here's the thing to understand: ideas are cheap and easy. It's not all that tough to come up with a hundred ideas on any given topic, but frankly we neither need nor want a hundred ideas. At any given point in time, we only need one or two really good ideas, and then we need to actually do something with them. Stormdraining is a practice that can help move us in that direction.

Stormdraining is more than just the inverse of ideation. It can even be performed apart from a brainstorming session, to get rid of all sorts of clutter. So if you're looking at a thirty-pound requirements document or a process diagram the size of house, a stormdraining session can help winnow things down to a more reasonable size. Want to try it? Great—here are the rules:

1. EVERYTHING IS ON THE TABLE

No sacred cows, please. If you brainstormed it, wrote it, or made it, it's fair game for going down the drain. So don't make a list of set-aside items that are too big for the drain. If you do, then start by draining that particular part of the swamp.

2. DELETE IS THE DEFAULT

When brainstorming, the objective is to create and add, so our default mode is creative and additive. It's all about more, more, more. Not sure if something is worth writing down? That's all right; write it down anyway.

Stormdraining is just the reverse. The purpose is to remove and subtract, so just like brainstorming's rule that every idea goes on the board, when stormdraining we must turn the pencil around and make liberal use of the eraser. Not sure if something should be deleted? Only one way to find out—erase that sucker and see what happens.

Because we've trained ourselves to value adding things, when we propose sending item 3 down the drain, the natural response is to justify its existence and argue for its retention. Resist that urge. Instead, accept each deletion as proposed. Train your brain to work in a new way. This gets easier with practice, which is sort of the whole point.

3. BUILD ON OTHER PEOPLE'S DELETIONS

This rule parallels the brainstorming guideline of building on other people's ideas. For example, if someone suggests building an airplane without a pilot, then it probably doesn't need that ejection seat. Or the oxygen system. Or the glass canopy. Remember, we're trying to reduce quantity and hone in on the essentials. Your teammate's suggestion to remove one thing most likely points to other parts that can also be removed.

4. MAKE IT FUN

Celebrate and encourage the deletions. Encourage and praise people's creativity and courage when they propose sending something down the drain. One of the things stormdraining aims to do is modify the mental programming we've all received through years of brainstorming. As we learn to release endorphins in response to a deletion, we increase our capacity to pursue elegant simplicity in other situations, and reduce our susceptibility to engage in misguided bloat. The fun part is essential; don't skip it.

5. WHEN YOU DELETE SOMETHING,
REALLY DELETE IT.

Don't set it aside and save it for posterity. Don't take a photo to preserve the moment. Erase it. Drain it. Disencumber yourself from it. Make it go away. And then revel in your freedom from the thing. If it is actually good and valuable, it will return on its own. Nobody forgets a truly good idea. If the thing is valuable, it'll pop back up again, I promise.

But hold on. What if we do this stormdraining thing and then have nothing left? What if everything drains away? Actually, that outcome is nothing to worry about, and in the unlikely event it does happen, it's probably cause for celebration (see rule 4). If the original list contained truly good and important ideas, they will either stick around or reemerge. And in the unlikely event that we are left with a blank whiteboard at the end of the hour, maybe that tells us something about the material we were working with in the first place. While it may be uncomfortable to discover that nothing from our brainstorming session was worth keeping, it is better to be aware of this situation right away instead of remaining blissfully, dangerously ignorant. A return to emptiness may be exactly what the team needs.

Just as brainstorming is not about throwing stupid ideas on the wall and contentedly keeping every single one, stormdraining is not merely about permanently sweeping everything away, good and bad alike, and blindly accepting each deletion.

Instead, stormdraining is a brain hack that aims to

shift our perception and judgment. It trains us to see that streamlining, simplifying, and reducing are all positive steps in the design process. They make the final product better and thus should be celebrated and valued as much as any addition.

Stormdraining encourages reductive thinking patterns, creating meaning through subtraction, like when a block of granite is carved into a statue. A master sculptor knows there is no need to keep all those little chips of stone. They are rightly swept up and disposed of. What truly matters is the sculpted object itself. Let's take a closer look at the practice of sculpture, beginning with sculpture's little brother, whittling.

Reductive Thinking

As a young Boy Scout, I tried my hand at whittling once or twice and managed to produce a respectable pile of wood-chips on several occasions. Alas, a career as a highly paid professional wood-carver was not in the cards for me, so I dedicated my attention to other aspects of scoutcraft, like making fires and learning to administer first aid to cuts and burns.

Now, a million years later, I find myself thinking back to those days of hiking, camping, and picking ashes out of my dinner. Specifically, I've got whittling on my mind. I may not have ever finished carving that wolf head out of bass-wood, but I just might have learned a lesson anyway. It just took a while for me to realize I'd learned it.

When we think about making something, the creative activities that come to mind are generally additive. Writing software? That involves creating lines of code, assembling modules, and generally increasing the program's file size.

Want to build a monkey bridge with your fellow scouts? You'll need to gather some big logs and lots of rope. Start by lashing two logs together, then a third and a fourth. Eventually, you'll add rope, rope, and more rope. Voilà— monkey bridge complete!

What these activities have in common is a reliance on adding as the primary creative mechanism. Whittling is different. Whittlers start with a block of material, then create by removing and disposing, first cutting away large pieces, then narrowing in on detail work and finally sanding off the rough spots. At least, that's what I'm told. Like I said, I never quite finished my whittling project.

Unlike the first log of our monkey bridge or the first line of computer code, the block we're carving contains all the atoms of the final product. Sure, the kids who finish their whittling projects may decide to add paint or varnish later (show-offs!), but the majority of the whittler's creation occurs via subtraction from initial conditions rather than addition. My failure as a whittler means I didn't remove enough from that block of wood, not that I didn't add enough.

Awareness of this approach expands our creative repertoire and introduces opportunities to come at a design problem from a different angle. Specifically, it introduces a mode of problem solving called reductive thinking. To learn more about it, we turn to StoneProject.org, a wonderful website run by a group of Scottish sculptors from the Edinburgh College of Art.

As the site explains, "The additive approach is so pervasive that it has a monopoly on almost every discipline." This won't do. The Stone Project sculptors aim to break up the monopoly by introducing the subtractive practice of reductive thinking; they seek to develop "a general principle of carving," and to help people see it is possible to "trim a world into existence." This is not an attempt to replace the more common additive approaches but rather to augment them.

Carving, sculpting, whittling—these are powerful metaphors for how the FIRE approach works, and because they are largely underused approaches, they have great potential to awaken new insights simply by pointing us toward unexplored territory.

Simplicity is at the core of FIRE, and simplification generally involves reducing something to its core elements. In the same way, a sculptor chisels away all the marble that is not part of the desired shape. To paraphrase the great Michelangelo, a tool—a knife, hammer, saw, or chisel—is applied for the express purpose of removing and revealing the figure previously encased in the marble or wood.

And yet, for all its focus on removal, sculpture is not demolition. We may produce a pile of wood chips or stone dust in the process, but that pile of sweepings is not the goal; the sculpted object is. And the best sculptures retain a link to their source, reveling in the natural flow of the material, the knots and whorls of wood, the streaks and ribbons of marble. As the Stone Project writers explain, "the qualities that a raw material possesses are elements to be preserved." Yes, sculpting is reductive. It is also preservative. The key to mastery lies in knowing what to reduce and what to preserve.

The reduction brings to mind the R in FIRE. A block of marble or wood starts big, and then gets smaller as we get closer to the final product. This experience of shrinking toward completion is quite different from the way we usually measure progress. Software programmers who proudly point to ever-increasing source lines of code (SLOC) count as their primary indication of progress may do well to look with a sculptor's eye. Same for any writer who assesses quality by simply counting the words or pages produced.

Measuring the value of a program in terms of lines of code or a document in terms of its page count is a bit like assessing the artistic merits of a sculpture in terms of how much it weighs. This might be an interesting measurement, and it is certainly objective and scientific, but a statue's poundage or a program's SLOC count tells us very little about how good or bad the thing is. Bear in mind, a finished statue weighs *less* than the block from which it was carved, not more, so even if we want to use weight as a measure of completion, we probably should not expect to see the weight increase over time.

Because sculpted materials can be expensive and unforgiving, and because a cut cannot easily be undone, many sculptors build a model out of a pliable material like clay before they begin carving. The model allows them to explore and experiment with forms and shapes without having to consume large quantities of expensive stone. This approach minimizes the cost and reminds us that thrift is an important part of the process.

Unlike carving, modeling is largely additive; bits of clay are pressed onto a form, then shaped and reshaped. Model building follows "the logic of assembly," to borrow another Stone Project phrase, adding pieces to create a coherent whole. In contrast, the subsequent sculpting follows a different type of logic—the logic of reduction. This echoes the behavior described in the simplicity cycle, as shown in figure 7.3.

On a technology development project, one of the most obvious places to apply the sculptor's logic is in the area of documentation. When we are handed a 300-page document template before any content is added, perhaps we should reach for a chisel before reaching for a pen.

While it certainly takes time and wisdom to craft a tightly focused, well-sculpted report, budget, schedule, or plan, the final product is likely to save much time and effort in the long run. Sculpting may not feel fast in the moment, but the clarity it brings to the effort facilitates the project's overall speed. Smaller documents require less time to read, review, coordinate, and approve. They communicate more clearly and make it easier for people to find the information they need. This increases understanding and helps us make timely decisions rather than getting lost and delayed in an endless labyrinth of paper.

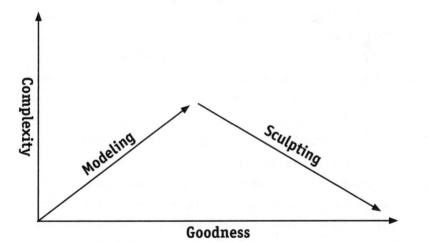

FIGURE 7.3. MODELING VERSUS SCULPTING

The Stone Project writers explain that "the triumphant sculptor is the liberator," and so it is with FIRE. Adopting the practice of reductive thinking helps us liberate ourselves and our teams from the tangles that result from purely additive practices. As with all new approaches, learning to think like a sculptor will require some effort, but the basic principle is easy enough to grasp and apply. The first step is to recognize that the additive mind-set's monopoly can be broken. Then we can reach for the chisel or blade that will reveal a hidden masterpiece.

Steampunk

Okay, confession time. For all my comments about the virtues of simplicity, I have to admit my inordinate fondness for the Victorian futurist brand of science fiction known as steampunk. I go absolutely gaga over its convoluted contraptions full of gears, pipes, and tubes, populated by characters in vests, hats, and goggles. In stories and images alike, steampunk presents a delightful complexity full of rich layers that I find compelling. It is riveting to watch the Improbable Clockwork Duke and his inventor friend Lady Chesterton of Surrey, Mistress of the Skies, fly their brass dirigible over London as they do battle with the demented Doctor Pneumatic, and not only because both sides use so many rivets. From an aesthetic point of view there is something profoundly satisfying about all that texture. Even in its excess, I can't get enough.

Because of my long-standing devotion to simplicity, my attraction to steampunk was hard to understand at first. How could I possibly justify liking something so complicated? Over time, I realized a large part of the genre's appeal comes from the fact that it is historical, and we are viewing works in progress. Every artifact is immature, even primitive. Each is an exploration and experiment, moving toward a future we currently inhabit. This means modern readers and viewers approach steampunk from a position of design sophistication. With steampunk we already know what lies ahead—simplifying improvements—but it is great fun to watch this early stage of the journey.

Speaking of great fun, the best steampunk novel I ever read is actually a work of nonfiction, not a novel at all. Titled *Progress in Flying Machines*, it was written by an American railway bridge engineer named Octave Chanute. This epic work, first published in 1894, chronicles almost four hundred years of failed aviation experiments, from Leonardo da Vinci to Chanute's own contemporaries. When Wilbur Wright asked the Smithsonian Institution for reference material on aeronautics, this is the book they recommended.

Progress is real-life steampunk, full of brass-plated clockworks, engines that run on gunpowder, and imaginative artifacts that would not seem out of place at your local steampunk convention, such as the 1864 apparatus with five pairs of flapping wings designed by Gustave de Struve and Nicolas de Telescheff (see figure 7.4).

For such an old and often technical book (there are numerous tables, calculations, and diagrams throughout), *Progress* is remarkably readable today, and frequently funny. In one memorably generous phrase Chanute describes the accomplishment of a French locksmith named Besnier who, in 1687, "took short downward flights aided by gravity." I'm pretty sure that's a polite way to describe falling, and I think I detect a wink and nod in Chanute's prose. However, that phrasing is an exception. For the most part, Chanute pulls no punches, as when he calls the result

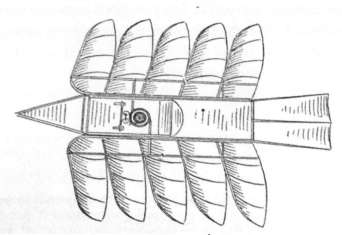

FIGURE 7.4. STRUVE AND TELESCHEFF'S FLYING MACHINE

of one Mr. De Groof's 1864 experiment "disastrous," when he summarizes a particular set of experiments by saying "all of these are worthless," or when he acknowledges that "almost all experiments with aeroplanes have hitherto been flat failures."

Chanute captures great and even personal detail about humanity's many attempts to launch into the wild blue yonder. He recounts the story of an aeronaut named Degen who in 1812 went to Paris to demonstrate an apparatus involving flapping wings and a small balloon. When strong winds blew him away for the third time and prevented him from ascending to the skies, he was "beaten unmercifully and laughed at afterwards" by the disappointed Parisians. Beaten *and* laughed at? Ouch! Yet such is the fate of an unsuccessful aeronaut circa 1812.

In what is perhaps the most steampunkesque scene in the book, Chanute tells the story of an "aerial locomotive" experiment performed in 1784 by one Mr. F. D. Artingstall.

This real-life attempt to build a flying train propelled by flapping wings worked about as well as could be expected: "When steam was turned on the wings worked vigorously, but the machine jerked up and down, rushed from side to side, and, in fact, performed all kinds of gymnastic movements except flight. This experiment was terminated by the explosion of the boiler."

What I wouldn't give to have seen that experiment in person. I desperately hope someone turns Chanute's book into a movie. I hereby nominate Morgan Freeman as narrator.

Despite the widespread reliance on steam power during his time, Chanute hinted at the possibility of a different future, writing, "Steam-engines, therefore, seem to have been so much reduced in weight as to admit of their being employed as motors for flying machines. They may not be a final solution, for it may be that some form of gas or petroleum engine will prove to be still better adapted to aerial purposes." And indeed, the Wright brothers designed and built a gasoline engine for their successful aircraft, leaving the age of steam behind.

Along with his suspicion that gas might someday replace steam, Chanute offers a few additional clues about what attributes a successful mechanism must eventually demonstrate. The most prominent of these attributes is simplicity. Chanute quotes one Mr. R. C. Jay of the British Aeronautical Society, who in 1877 explained that despite "a great many experiments, he had not yet succeeded in making a propeller (wings) sufficiently simple and effective for practical purposes."

Note the phrase "sufficiently simple." Even during the age when steampunk technology was the state of the art, some practitioners and experimenters understood the value of simplicity and sought to counter the prevailing preference for complexity. This theme of simplicity pops up throughout the book, and one can feel the sense of frustration and hope in Chanute's voice as he recognizes the need for simpler mechanisms and bemoans the aviation community's persistent inability to produce them. In one particularly poignant passage, Chanute writes about "the difficult design of a simple form," acknowledging how challenging it is to reduce a design to its essential elements.

This desire for simplicity is perhaps why Chanute lavishes his highest praise on an Australian inventor named Hargrave, writing, "If there be one man, more than another, who deserves to succeed in flying through the air, that man is Mr. Laurence Hargrave, of Sydney, New South Wales." Hargrave was most famous for designing a box kite capable of lifting a man into the air, although his contributions to aviation went far beyond kites. He also experimented with steam engines powered by alcohol as well as engines whose motive force was provided by compressed air or "twisted strings of india-rubber" (aka rubber bands). In commenting on one of the Australian's engines, Chanute calls it "a marvel of simplicity and lightness," then goes on to quote a letter from Hargrave in which he foreshadows the FIRE approach, writing, "my constant endeavors are directed to making the machines simple and cheap." Where most of his predecessors and contemporaries used increasingly complex mechanisms to produce lift and/or propulsion, Hargrave stood almost alone as a grand simplifier. By all accounts his successful orientation away from complexity influenced Orville and Wilbur greatly.

Other clues to future success are scattered throughout

the book. Chanute points out that on both land and sea the rotary motion of train wheels and paddlewheels is superior to the back-and-forth "reciprocating action" of legs and oars. He then predicts "that some rotating device shall be found the preferable propeller, should aerial navigation ever be accomplished." Chanute justified his prediction by explaining that continuous circular motion is simpler and more efficient, noting that "the strains of a rotating apparatus will be less destructive than those involving reversals of motion." Indeed, today's propellers and jet engines alike spin rather than flap, confirming his hunch. Chanute even got some of today's terminology correct, as in the chapter titled "Screws to Lift and Propel," where he wrote about "Penaud's flying screw, which is called by the French a 'Hélicoptère.'"

Whether we're talking about fictional steampunk or the genre's real-life inspiration, the thing that is so right about this technology is that it is so wrong. As outside observers, we know each brass-and-steam mechanism is a stepping-stone to a simpler future, not a final answer. We can appreciate all the excessive effort involved when characters try to produce miracles without microchips because we know a more efficient solution is just around the corner. The resulting improbable machines delight us with their ornamental complexity and amuse us with their functional limitations. Even apart from technology, steampunk fashion fascinates by the richness of the layers—vests, goggles, pipes, hats, and walking sticks, all of which are stripped away in today's casual jeans and T-shirt culture. While modern clothing is more comfortable and easier to wear, the steampunk outfits are so cool looking that I feel something was lost along the way.

The other thing that is so right is the way steampunk

designs reveal and revel in a machine's inner workings, the gears and belts and tubes that end up on the outside of the device rather than safely tucked away beneath a sleekly sterile modern plastic skin. A large part of steampunk's appeal is no doubt attributable to this contrast, this transparent alternative to today's opacity. Showing the inner gear works gives steampunk technology a degree of accessibility unmatched by an iPod. The reader can imagine wrestling with pipes and levers. It is much harder to even understand a black box component where the workings are hidden and would be too small to touch even were the cover removed, let alone envision ourselves racing to repair it before Doctor Pneumatic's replicating mechanical minions overrun the Tower of London again.

Steampunk reminds us that simplicity and complexity come in different flavors. Superficial simplicity can be shallow and boring, while a more thoughtfully simple design captivates. Similarly, complexity can be engaging and rewarding if done well, while excessive complexity is confusing and off-putting. Because these are aesthetic considerations, they are subject to variations of taste. One person's slick elegance strikes another as coldly barren, while one person's off-putting clutter is another's rich texture. Understanding the reasons behind the decisions can increase our appreciation of the final result, but even if we don't recognize or agree with the reasoning, understanding that such reasons exist can help us apprehend the appeal of the thing.

So, for all the talk about simplicity as sophistication, let us also remember that complexity has a value as well as a cost. The FIRE emphasis on elegant simplicity does not mean that there is no place for complexity—even excessive complexity—particularly if it is part of a continuing journey toward a more mature outcome. As the simplicity cycle section explained, we cannot move directly from immature simplicity to mature simplicity. We must first wrestle with the intermediate phase of complexity. That is precisely what steampunk invites us to do.

Whether the design is simple or complex, we ultimately crave *coherence*. What matters is that the object hangs together in a unified whole. Complexity tends to reduce coherence, which is one of the reasons FIRE emphasizes the pursuit of simplicity, but a well-designed steampunk artifact conveys a certain gestalt and a sense of purposefulness. There is a feeling of wholeness about the Extraordinary Clockwork Duke's ensemble, with his velvet vest concealing his brass heart, the Prismatic Seven-Lensed Microtelescopic Goggles allowing him to see ethereal flows, and the ever-present, always-unreliable Plasmatic Disruptor Pistol strapped to his leg holster.

All this is to say that both simplicity and complexity have an aesthetic appeal and even an operational value. Despite FIRE's clear preference for simplicity, there is something to be said for occasionally building a steam-powered, brass-plated, telescoping perambulator. Just don't let Doctor Pneumatic get his diabolical hands on it, because if he does, we're all doomed.

So, if steampunk illustrates the *value* of complexity, let's take a closer look at what complexity *costs*.

The Dishwasher: A True Story

This really happened.

Several years ago, my wife and I were in the market for a new dishwasher, an indisputable sign that adulthood was upon us. After performing the requisite due diligence with the latest issue of *Consumer Reports*, we visited the appliance department of a local retailer and considered our options in person.

After a thorough assessment, in which we considered everything from noise level to color, we made our choice and flagged down Tom the sales representative to close the deal.

Tom nodded sagely at our selection, complimented our taste, wrote some mysterious numbers on a scrap of paper, and then directed our attention to the dishwasher right next to the one we'd selected. This machine was the same make and looked almost identical to the one we'd picked. It only cost fifty dollars more.

"Let me just show you folks this feature," Tom said in the slightly conspiratorial tone of someone who knows a secret and, because he is your best friend, wants to share it with you. "Check out the top rack."

With a practiced flourish, he swung the dishwasher door open, slid the top rack out, and then paused dramatically.

"Do you ever cook a large meal, like on Thanksgiving"—he asked as music swelled dramatically in his mind—"and end up with big dishes that don't fit in the top of the dishwasher?"

What answer could we give other than yes? I could not recall ever being in this situation, but I easily imagined it could happen in some hypothetical future, so I nodded. Plus, I think I must have been a little bit hypnotized or something.

With a wink, a nod, a grin, and a flick of his wrist, Tom the King of All Dishwasher Salesmen pressed a lever or pulled a tab or slid a stopper or activated whatever mysterious mechanism was necessary to . . . wait for it . . . lower the top rack by an inch or two.

Grinning broadly and perhaps perspiring lightly, Tom turned to us in triumph. "The top rack raises and lowers, to accommodate larger items."

And this must-have feature increased the price by only fifty dollars! Clearly, we would be fools to pass up an opportunity to bring such an important piece of new technology into our home. Resisting the urge to shout, "We'll take two!" my wife and I nodded our approval and became the proud owners of a top-quality dishwasher with an adjustable top rack.

For the whole time we owned that dishwasher—which did a fine job cleaning our dishes, by the way—we never moved that rack out of its original position. Not up. Not down. Not once.

Okay, that's a bit of a silly story. It is small beer compared to things like stealth jets and spaceships, but it demonstrates on a micro scale what happens when we make design or purchase decisions based on hypothetical futures rather than actual performance needs. Plus, I suspect most readers will remember this stupid dishwasher story long after the NASA examples are forgotten.

Let's take a look at what happened here, beginning with the fact that in my entire life I had never once encountered a situation in which I thought to myself, "I wish that dish rack was higher (or lower)," nor did I ever find myself saying, "I'd pay fifty dollars more for a rack that goes up and down!" The new feature Tom sold us so confidently was an unanticipated bonus, a capability I'd never before needed and, it turns out, would never use.

If things always worked out that way, angry villagers

would have run Tom out of town by now, but of course things occasionally turn out differently. Sometimes the new, unexpected feature is exactly what we need, which means Steve Jobs was probably correct when he said it is not the customers' job to know what they want. There are plenty of cases where new and unanticipated features, introduced to us by Tom and his brethren on showroom floors across the country, genuinely make our lives better, easier, or safer.

So, the point here is *not* that developers or shoppers must have a perfect crystal ball view of every future contingency and should only design or purchase new stuff that is exactly aligned with needs we are consciously aware of. There is no need to reject every additional feature Tom tells us about simply because we hadn't thought of it in advance. Such all-or-nothing thinking is unnecessarily narrow. The point of this increasingly goofy story is to make sure we put a little thought into the question of price and necessity.

Maybe you can't live without your adjustable dishwasher rack. Maybe you move yours up and down every morning and twice on Sunday, thereby avoiding hours of sudsy drudgery at the sink, which means you now have time to learn to paint with watercolors, go for long walks on the beach with people you love, and of course write the Great American Novel so that you can experience all the fame and fortune that society showers upon its most beloved authors.

But not me. For me, that was fifty dollars I didn't need to spend on a feature I promptly forgot all about, if the truth be told. Why, then, did I buy it? For starters, it was only fifty bucks, an amount of money I could spend without a noticeable degradation of the lifestyle to which I'd become accustomed. Second, a dishwasher is a long-term commitment. Once it's installed, we can't easily swap it out for a new model. So if this extra feature was even potentially interesting, we had to get it now. Adding it later wasn't an option.

Which brings us (finally!) to the main point: People love features. Features sell. In fact, consumer research shows that when given a choice between two similar products—cameras, dishwashers, and the like—shoppers generally prefer to pay a little extra for a product with more features. Further research shows that the vast majority of these extra features go completely unused. Apparently people prefer features before the sale, not after. This means the main purpose of all these extra widgets is to sell the product rather than to serve the customer's interests. In the case of software, for example, researcher Jim Johnson reports that "64% of the features [in software programs] are never or rarely used." It's nice to know my dishwasher and I have company.

This tells me commercial product designers have an excuse for their tendency toward feature overload. It's what the market prefers at the point of sale. Fewer features equal fewer sales, which presumably means fewer profits. That's something to keep in mind.

But here's the twist: while the market generally prefers lots of features, most of the time that is not what the customer wants or needs once he or she gets the thing home and takes it out of the box. This means maybe—just *maybe*—it's occasionally advisable to take a simpler, more streamlined design approach. It might even be possible to make a profit while doing so. And you know who's really good at doing that? Apple.

Critics went absolutely nuts when Apple announced that

the battery on the iPod was not replaceable. How could Steve Jobs live with himself after failing to provide consumers with such a basic feature as a replaceable battery? What was he thinking? There's no way a company can make a profit with products like this. How arrogant! How stupid! How unresponsive to customer desires! Everybody knows customers absolutely love to change the battery in their portable music devices. When I was a kid, I changed the batteries in my Walkman every day, whether they needed it or not. How dare Mr. Jobs take this pleasure away from us?

And yet, Apple managed to squeak by and occasionally produced profits that were significantly higher than the total profits of the next six largest Internet and technology companies combined. The numbers change constantly, but in the four quarters leading up to November 2012, Apple made $41 billion while Microsoft, eBay, Google, Yahoo, Facebook, and Amazon together made $34 billion. I suppose that's interesting if you're into that sort of thing.

Clearly, a lack of changeable batteries didn't get in the way of brisk business. And that's not the only thing Apple left out of its devices.

True story: a complete stranger once approached me in a parking lot and sheepishly handed me an iPod. This older gentleman explained that he'd borrowed the device from his great-great-great-grandchild in order to listen to his favorite band (I like to imagine it was They Might Be Giants) but now he was done listening and couldn't figure out how to turn the darn thing off.

With a confident smile, I agreed to give the poor gent a hand. After all, I'm an engineer and a young person with 20/20 vision. And I'm an Eagle Scout. Helping people is what I do. Sure, I'd never owned an iPod, but how hard could it be to locate the off switch, right? As it turns out, pretty hard. After a fairly thorough investigation, I couldn't find the power button either and was equally sheepish as I apologized and handed it back to him, still on and playing a song. I later found out that model does not have an on/off button. How ya like them Apples?

Sometime later, I purchased my first Apple product—a first-generation iPod Shuffle. You know, the kind that looks like a pack of gum. This particular model does have a power switch, but not much else. There is no display, so the only way to tell what song is playing is to listen to the earbuds. The only way to find out what song is next is . . . to listen to the earbuds. It doesn't come with games, an address book, a scroll wheel, a calendar, an alarm clock, or any of that stuff. Basically, the only thing it does is play music in random order. And you know what? That's perfect. I bought it in 2006 and still use it when I'm running on the treadmill in 2014. It works fine. And I've never once changed the battery—partly because I can't but mostly because I've never needed to.

When FIRE sets a firm budget limit and encourages us to spend less, it is an attempt to prevent us from paying extra to design or purchase new features that will never get used. A tight spending profile means every dollar has to count, so before we pay a little more for that adjustable rack or full-color screen on a two-inch device, we should make sure it is worth the expense.

In the case of the dishwasher, Tom's words should have clued us in. His proposed scenario was a big Thanksgiving dinner, which happens once or twice a year at most, unless we go to Grandma's house that year, in which case the dishwasher in my kitchen won't be any help at all. On the occasional year when we do Thanksgiving at home, we can probably wash by hand any dishes too large for the machine.

In a similar fashion, the emphasis on simplicity and restraint encourages us to avoid adding bells and whistles— particularly those that are rarely used and that perform functions that could be achieved by existing mechanisms.

That last point is key. It's a good idea to pay fifty bucks for a feature if there is no other way to accomplish an important task, even if the task only has to be done once or twice a year. But if the hand washing option exists, we might be better off saving our money. Bear in mind, the hand washing option almost always exists.

There is a balance to hit, of course. Certain additions are genuinely necessary and important, fulfilling needs that may have been previously unexpressed. Nobody wants to be the guy who says "Seat belts? What do you want those for? They just clutter up the driving experience." But before you let Tom the Salesman (or Tom the Designer) convince you to spend an extra fifty dollars on an adjustable dishwasher rack, spend a few minutes thinking about what you're really paying for.

Icons

Long before it built iPods without power buttons and display screens, Apple carefully cultivated a culture of restraint and simplicity. This was expressed in its products as well as its advertisements and internal business practices. One particularly instructive instance is the way Apple used icons as simplifiers.

They are ubiquitous now, but when Susan Kare began designing computer icons for Apple in the early 1980s, the idea of using a tiny pictograph as a navigation tool was a relatively novel innovation. One of Kare's most famous designs is the pixelated, black-and-white "Happy Mac" that greeted Apple users until it was replaced in 2002. It is an image familiar even to non–Mac users, so no wonder she picked it for the cover of her 2011 book simply titled *Icons*.

As computer users of a certain age recall, the alternative to a clickable icon was the DOS command prompt. This text-based approach required moving through a series of levels and keeping track of the location of each executable file.

Want to play *Tetris* on your PC, circa 1990? No problem. From the C:\ drive, just type "cd games," followed by "cd tetris" to enter the Tetris folder embedded in your game folder. Then, presuming the game file is named tetris.exe, just type in "tetris" and hit return. Voilà—hours of spatial-orientation fun awaits!

An icon does away with all those steps. Using icons, *Tetris* is just a click or two away. If you played *Tetris* as often as I did, I think you'll agree a picture would have truly been worth a thousand words.

We could spend some time examining the relative merits of icon-based approaches and text-based structures, but I think the consensus is clear on that one, so let's not. Instead, how about we take a look at the way Kare describes her creations and see what we can learn?

In a profile for *Wired* magazine, Kare refers to icons as "a visual shorthand," a simplified representation of a more complex reality. She goes on to explain the simplicity of her icons, noting that "visual complexity is not necessarily directly proportional to effectiveness."

This concept of the relationship between complexity

and effectiveness is widely acknowledged in theory—and widely ignored in practice. Designers of all stripes have a deep-seated tendency to try to increase the value of their design—be it in art, technology, writing, or education—by making the thing more complex. Kare's icons remind us of what we supposedly already know and they challenge us to seek the simpler path.

By their simple functionality, Kare's designs disprove the more-is-better myth. Her work shows that simplicity correlates with clarity, a principle with applicability far beyond the realm of icon design. Each one is a micromasterpiece, a handcrafted monument in miniature, and each demonstrates a profound understanding of how the mind works.

Like any well-designed product, Kare's icons have a slightly inevitable feel to them, as if she merely documented the most obvious way to portray a particular concept. This is certainly not the case. In the hands of a less disciplined designer, these icons could have been far more complex and far less useful.

Kare's images are never inadvertently simple, nor regretfully so. Instead, the simplicity of each is deliberate and cherished. Further, while her early work found a home on black-and-white screens with limited resolution, her recent stuff focuses on "graphics for screens with limited real estate," embracing a different set of limitations. Although computer technology advanced and placed more colors on her palette and more pixels at her disposal, Kare and her studio partners "continued to optimize for clarity and simplicity."

These days, her work features plenty of color, but on any given piece she uses a decidedly restrained palette. The (brief!) biography at Kare.com explains that "just because millions of colors are available, every one need not be used in every icon." This restraint is not only an indication of her artistic sensibility but also reveals a deep commitment to practical utility. Simpler icons are simultaneously more artistic and more useful.

Kare's designs are both pleasing to the eye and practical, a delicate balance to hit. This balance represents a mutually reinforcing relationship between art and commerce, between the needs for capability and clarity. The artistic nature of her simple little designs makes them easier to understand and remember, while their utility further adds to their appeal. One need not be an artist to learn something from her example.

Speaking of appeal, Kare frequently uses humor to enhance memorability, explaining that "cute beats edgy." Humans have an easier time recognizing and remembering the meaning behind a funny little icon than behind a blander version. Like simplicity, the wit exhibited by her icons is the result of conscious effort. Her work shows the value and importance of humor, an important lesson for anyone who thinks serious business is incompatible with smiling.

For all their simplicity, wit, and grace, perhaps the most remarkable aspect of her icons is their longevity. Kare's work has a tendency to remain in use far longer than one might expect from something so small and simple. The Happy Mac, for example, was used for almost twenty years. Kare explains that good icons "need not be frequently redesigned," so along with providing simple and effective functionality, a good icon also saves time and money by avoiding frequent redos.

The efficient blend of simplicity and thrift in Kare's icons is an easy target to miss, particularly if we don't aim for it the way she does. If we treat complexity as a sign of sophistication and try to apply every color in the rainbow to every design, we will never even approach the clarity, effectiveness, and longevity of her work. Fortunately, her example is all around us, serving to guide those who are willing to follow. So the next time you come across an icon, give it a little thought. Look for signs of simplicity, brevity, and humor. Then look for ways to apply these principles to your own designs, whatever those designs may be.

We now turn to Jolly Old England, where we'll meet a remarkably talented software programmer who put all these lessons together and produced some truly impressive results.

The Health and Safety Information System

Suppose you're on a train and you suddenly *must* know who won the Olympic gold medal for tug-of-war in 1908. No problem. After a brief consultation with the mobile device of your choice, you'll learn it was a team of City of London policemen. Interestingly, British policemen won all three tug-of-war medals that year, with Liverpool bobbies taking silver and the Metropolitan Police K Division taking bronze. Check it yourself if you want to.

In our increasingly Google-ized reality, we take for granted that all the world's information is immediately available at all times via devices that fit in our pockets. We never need to wonder who won an obscure sporting event from a hundred years ago. So, when the British Ministry of Defence (MoD) sought to create an online library of safety data sheets for hazardous material handling guidelines, it didn't sound like a very difficult task. How hard can it be to create a searchable library of PDFs? And didn't they have one of those already? Unfortunately, this challenge quickly shaped up to be very difficult indeed.

When the MoD asked for bids to replace the manpower-intensive legacy system, they received an unpleasant bit of sticker shock. Price estimates were in the range of £7 million. That was a nonstarter. Something else had to be done.

Enter Allen Woods. Refusing to accept that a good solution was necessarily expensive and complex, and blissfully unaware of the higher bids, he produced the MoD's Health and Safety Information System (HSIS) for £65,000, literally 1 percent of the other bidders' price. It went live on October 1, 2008, and the annual maintenance cost is now less than one-tenth of the previous manual system. No toy, the HSIS is "more accurate, faster and . . . more comprehensive" than the system it replaced. It is "one of the busiest policy and governance sites on the Defence Intranet," receiving upwards of 400,000 queries per year. It bears repeating that the system was delivered for less than 1 percent of the original price estimate. While a searchable PDF library of hazmat data sheets may not sound very sexy compared to other types of military technology, saving £6.9 million has an undeniable appeal.

What if the system didn't work? What if he had delivered a website that was entirely inadequate and unacceptable? This isn't what happened, of course, but it could have. In that case, the British government would have been exposed to a minimal loss of time and money, and would have been able to move on to plan B without much Sturm und Drang. Contrast this with the potential loss had it gone with one of the more expensive and slower proposals. Bear in mind, any approach can fail. Woods's approach succeeded, but if it had failed, the pain would have been negligible.

As with most of the stories and examples in this book, the primary message can be summed up in two words: this happened. And because it happened once, it could conceivably happen again. Awakening ourselves to the realm of new possibilities is a critical step toward making improvements. Naturally, we also want to learn something from this happening, to find some imitable practices and principles. This desire leads to the inevitable question, how is such a thing possible? How could Woods be so efficiently effective?

Those may be the obvious questions, but perhaps we should really be asking how those other bidders could possibly justify proposing solutions that cost two orders of magnitude more than Woods's system. Unfortunately, when presented with two wildly divergent prices, the natural reaction is to distrust the smaller number. Based on stories like this one, I suggest we may want to cultivate the habit of distrusting the larger one instead.

In a series of lengthy e-mails, Woods—who insisted I call him Allen—explained his approach. As I read his story, several things struck me. First, Allen is largely self-taught, which means he learned things he needed to know rather than things other people decided were important. This alignment between knowledge and need shielded him from distracting time-sinks and irrelevant rabbit trails. It's an eminently practical approach to education, and it has served him well.

Second, Allen spent a lot of time as an enlisted member of Her Majesty's Army—he was a staff sergeant when he left the service—which means he had a bench-level understanding of the mission rather than the more elevated, highly removed perspective of an academic or theoretician. This too is an admirable and desirable state of affairs.

And third, Allen has a terrific sense of humor, a trait he shares with all the most competent program managers and technologists I've known and worked with. Humor is often a shorthand for truth, and the same mind-set that converts profundity into laughs can also help us see through a project's clutter and focus in on the core mission. I wish all program managers and computer programmers were as profoundly funny as Allen. Their products and performance would no doubt be much improved. For that matter, so would the world.

Allen approached the challenge with speed, thrift, and simplicity at the forefront of his mind. He writes, "One of my continual concerns is how to do things at minimal cost. I use no third party components on anything I do (save one, there is a brilliant guy in New York who has produced a PDF component library. . . . I had to buy a license for $250 for a component that has worked without fault for five years, generating about half a million PDF files in that time—bloody clever that)."

Unlike his less enlightened competitors, Allen set out to build a website that did one or two things very well. This focus on a narrow set of priorities meant his final product was simpler to build, use, and maintain. Indeed, a 2010 case study of the HSIS explains that a need for minimal training was a key constraint on the design. "The solution would have to be simple to operate, even for the technically challenged," Allen notes, explaining that the user interface had to be "uncluttered and obvious."

If you have ever used a government website—or a commercial one, for that matter—you know how rare it is to find an uncluttered and obvious interface. I suspect the rarity of clarity is in large part caused by a failure to follow Allen's example of building solutions that can be operated by "the technically challenged." This deep commitment to simplicity also improved the system's reliability, since it had fewer components, fewer features, and fewer ways to break.

Allen explains that even before submitting his bid, he had "a considerable codebank" to draw from, which is one more example of the start-before-you-start heuristic. But while the final product made heavy use of existing code components, it was also an entirely new capability, tailored and suited for a particular need.

Allen's guiding principle is summed up in JFDI, which in polite language means, "Just focus and do it."

As he set out to "just f-ing do it," Allen made sure he focused on the most important features and capabilities. This meant his solution had to "comply with DII [Defence Information Infrastructure] technical standards" while also delivering "an increase in accuracy and a decrease in document production time." Accordingly, he followed a set of guiding constraints in terms of time, money, and complexity. These constraints led him to replace the legacy manual system with "a completely web enabled series of applications."

Now, the decision to migrate a manual service to the web might sound obvious, and so it is. No doubt the more expensive proposals also intended to put the system online, although I did not have access to those proposals so I can't speak with certainty. What I can confirm is that Allen's approach to web services was simple, speedy, and inexpensive. The other guys apparently had a rather high view of complexity and appeared to believe that a large price tag was a reliable indicator of quality.

Based on our correspondence, it is clear to me that Allen has a deep understanding of both the Internet and people. Even better, he knows how to effectively put the two together. While some web designers like to show off their mastery of obscure protocols and pack their products full of features that will never be used, Allen takes a wiser approach. His designs are simple, one might even say basic, but they do precisely what they need to do. When someone approaches the HSIS for the first time, a lack of familiarity with the system is no barrier to using it. I'd say the MoD more than got its money's worth. His site would have been a huge bargain at twice or even ten times the price.

The lesson we learn from Allen's story depends on our role. If we're the customer, maybe the lesson is to be skeptical of high bids rather than distrusting the low one. If we're the designer, maybe the lesson is about simplicity and focus, or building a code bank we can leverage for future projects. But regardless of where you sit, it is worth recognizing that a fast, inexpensive, restrained, and elegant option is almost always available.

The British Olympic team of 1908 was justifiably proud of dominating the tug-of-war competition. It took silver in 1912 and gold again in 1920, the last year the sport was included in the program. I know this because the Internet makes it so quick and easy to locate weird information. Of course, sometimes the Internet also makes it difficult and slow to locate information, particularly when web designers don't follow the example set by Allen Woods. But the best systems, like the HSIS, tend to be those developed on short timelines and tight budgets, using simple methods and a firm commitment to clarity.

We turn now from complexity to the question of speed and agility. Naturally, our inquiry into rapid, efficient movement begins at the intersection of Metropolis and a galaxy far, far away.

CHAPTER 8

Speed and Agility

Given the nature of the Internet and its denizens, it was only a matter of time before someone asked the question, "Who would win in a fight between Superman and the Death Star?" I know I always wondered about that, and fortunately the Internet thoroughly investigated the question and provided a definitive answer. A cure for cancer, on the other hand, remains sadly elusive.

The general consensus is that the Man of Steel has a clear advantage, although the prize for best answer ever goes to an Internet user named Thrumm who correctly responded, "Batman." I officially award negative ten points to all the commenters who turned the discussion into a comparison of the Star Wars movies and *Battlestar Galactica*, because if you're going to change the topic, at least have the decency to change it to Joss Whedon's show *Firefly*. Not because *Galactica* isn't awesome, but because *Firefly* is super-awesome. And yes, the *Serenity* could beat a Death Star any day of the week. Pardon me while I dial my nerd level back down from 11 . . .

The Superman/Death Star question is silly on several levels, which of course will not stop me from addressing it, just as the inherent silliness did not prevent 62 percent of my readers from putting down this book and Googling the answer already. The remaining 38 percent most likely participated in the discussion in the first place.

Obviously the question is silly because in the first Star Wars trilogy alone, Death Stars are repeatedly blown up by people with credentials far less impressive than the Son of Krypton's. Luke Skywalker is a half-trained Jedi when he takes out the first Death Star, a feat soon repeated by Lando Calrissian, who is a former city administrator flying a used cargo ship. Not only does Lando lack Superman's invulnerability and X-ray vision, he can't even use the Force. If Calrissian can do it, a better question might be, "Who *can't* beat a Death Star in a fight?" (Answer: Aquaman.)

Given its immense size and planet-busting firepower, the Death Star looks unstoppable. As the movies so aptly demonstrate (twice), it is anything but. Now, here's why the Death Star's doom is so completely believable and so immensely satisfying: agility beats strength every single time.

This means Superman doesn't beat the Death Star because he's so strong, although that helps. He wins because he's so fast. If the Death Star's laser jockeys can't hit the side of the *Millennium Falcon*, they are going to have an even harder time locking in on the smaller, more mobile guy in the red cape and tights.

There is a lesson in here for all of us, and nobody states it more succinctly than Jason Fried and David Hansson. In their book *Rework*, they write, "Quick wins." Quick as in speedy. As in fast. As in agile. As in Superman. That's what wins. The time when we could rely on sheer mass to ensure victory vanished a long, long time ago. The Death Star is dead. Long live the Man of Steel!

We may not be locked in existential combat with a literal Death Star, but chances are good our project is up against forces seeking to turn us to the Dark Side, to extend our schedules, expand our budgets, and make things more complicated. If I may mix my space sagas a bit, resistance sometimes feels futile.

Fortunately, there is hope. FIRE offers some ideas for maintaining agility in the face of overwhelming force. By exercising restraint, cultivating speed, keeping things small, and pursuing simplicity, we will find ourselves more agile than those who rely on bulk and complexity to get the job done. But the more we pile on features, functions, organizations, processes, documents, meetings, reports, delays, and extensions, the more we will become less agile and more vulnerable to that planet-busting superlaser.

Even if you are not fighting a moon-size space station, there are several advantages to being agile. For starters, speed reduces our exposure to change and helps maintain alignment between what we are building and what we need to build. If we spend ten years on a project, there's a pretty good chance the technology environment or the market will change. Worse yet, both will change, but in opposite directions. If we've locked in our design decisions and aren't able to adapt, we'll be in the same position as a Death Star against an agile opponent. If we haven't locked in the design, we'll find ourselves endlessly chasing a moving target, and when it comes to moving targets, it's better to be one than to aim for one. Speaking of which . . .

My amazing colleague and brother-in-arms Chris Quaid coined the term *moving target theory* to describe his über-agile approach to getting things done. The essence of his theory is succinctly captured in his personal motto, "Get in, get done, get gone before anyone knows you were there." Never content to rest on his laurels, Quaid operates somewhat like the Lone Ranger, riding off into the sunset at the end of each episode, after once again saving the day.

The idea behind moving target theory is that doing good work, particularly within a Death Star–esque bureaucracy or in the face of overwhelming firepower, requires speed and agility. This not only prevents unwarranted delays from getting in the way of delivering a product on time but also makes sure the corporate immune response does not identify you as an unwelcome foreign invader and try to eradicate you before you accomplish your mission. Or after you accomplish your mission, for that matter. Getting the job done is what matters, not protecting your place in the corporate hierarchy. Get in, get done, get gone.

Moving target theory (MTT) asserts that motion correlates with life, both now and in the future, and fast motion in particular. We move because we are alive, and that very movement is what keeps us alive. Accordingly, Quaid has developed a personal discipline of speed, refusing to tolerate or accommodate delays that many of us would accept as inevitable. In less skilled hands than his, this need for speed might thoughtlessly devolve into a manic, Tasmanian Devil whirl that is neither productive nor sustainable. Less-than-perceptive observers with a preference for deliberate sloth have been known to reach precisely this conclusion, but they are wrong. Quaid's clear-eyed focus on the mission ensures that his constant motion is headed in the right direction for the long haul. As someone who shared an office with him for a couple of years, I can confirm that his approach is more than a little contagious.

Quaid would be the first to assert that anyone can learn and use MTT. It's not complicated, it's not fancy, and it's not even that difficult. All it takes is commitment, imagination, energy, and guts. All it takes is the ability to see what needs to be done and a willingness to do it as quickly as possible, coupled with a willingness to move on to the next challenge when the first one is completed.

The late Colonel John Boyd's energy-maneuverability theory revolutionized aerial combat by reframing the way a fighter jet's performance is quantified. This fundamentally changed the way fighters were designed and the way they were flown. Similarly, Quaid's MTT concept offers a revolutionary approach to organizational behavior. Also like Boyd, Quaid's idea makes some people nervous, not only because it is unfamiliar but also because it sounds subversive.

MTT is built on an understanding that, to use Quaid's original spelling, a "buraecracy" is generally unable to recognize and acknowledge—or even tolerate—productive behavior that does not conform to predefined expectations, even if such behavior is explicitly and clearly supporting the organization's most important objectives. Is this truly subversive? Yes, but only to the people and structures that need to be subverted. MTT is actually *supportive* of the organization's deeper goals and objectives. However, it provides that support in unexpected ways, which is why the MTT practitioner must keep moving. In the context of a ponderous "buraecracy," this movement is a matter of professional survival as well as continued relevance.

In his epic book *The Fifth Discipline*, Peter Senge, a professor at the Massachusetts Institute of Technology, writes about the difference between commitment and compliance. Senge explains that compliance is overrated, while commitment, which is harder to establish and maintain, actually matters. Being an academic, Senge naturally uses more formal terminology (and lots of it) to make his point, but basically he suggests that compliance means doing what you're told, while commitment means doing what has to be done, whether you're told to do it or not. Quaid, being a self-proclaimed graduate of the *Saturday Night Live*-inspired Tonto, Frankenstein, and Tarzan School of Public Speaking, makes the same point as Senge but does so with his actions more than his words.

Senge and Quaid both teach us that commitment includes an element of initiative and creativity not found in compliance-based behavior. When someone is truly committed to an organization's goals, she is less likely to comply with the more arbitrary aspects of corporate normalcy. Instead, a moving target master fosters energetic, creative approaches to delivering mission success. For such people, satisfaction is based on what Henry David Thoreau called "success unexpected in common hours" rather than on simply meeting the standards and doing what they are told to do. Naturally, this gives corporate drones the vapors.

To be fair, those gassy compliance mavens are not entirely wrong. The end does not always justify the means, and some means are simply unjustifiable. Unfortunately, bureaucrats tend to get so caught up in official definitions and restrictions that they lose sight of the ends entirely. Because MTT is generally unexpected and surprising, they have a hard time recognizing its value or its ethics. In fact, Quaid's approach does not blindly tolerate any behavior so long as it is fast and well intentioned; it also needs to be aboveboard and ethical. Rule 1 of MTT is "Do the right thing, always."

Yes, we would do well to remember that even though historical and fictional villains alike tend to be firmly committed to their goals, their commitment does not qualify them as good role models. However, even the most cursory investigation of MTT or *The Fifth Discipline* reveals that the commitment Quaid and Senge are talking about is of an entirely different nature.

There's a reason I mention Chris Quaid in the same breath as Superman, John Boyd, and Peter Senge. He's just that good. His moving target theory may not have rigorous academic or mathematic credentials but it has something even better—two decades of real-life results. When I head out to do battle against a Death Star, there is no one I'd rather have on my side than my buddy Quaid.

"Oh, Boy . . ."

Our exploration into agility now moves to the small screen and a television show that premiered in 1989 and ran for five seasons. The show was *Quantum Leap*, and even though it's been off the air for more than twenty years, it is still one of the coolest sci-fi shows ever made. The only conceivable way it could have been more awesome is if *Firefly*'s Nathan Fillion was in it, but who knows what sort of unintended consequences might have befallen that beloved-but-canceled show in the altered reality in which the casting director picked Fillion instead of Scott Bakula for the lead role. If time travel stories teach us anything, it's to leave the past alone. Scott Bakula, your legacy is safe.

In the unlikely event that someone unfamiliar with the

show is still reading this, let me briefly explain *Quantum Leap*'s structure, starting with the end. At the conclusion of each episode, we see the leaper Sam Beckett, having successfully resolved that week's drama, taking possession of a stranger's body (i.e., "leaping") somewhere in the past, generally at a moment of peril. This set the stage for next week's show and inevitably elicited a worried "Oh, boy . . ." from Sam just before the credits rolled. If you're still feeling confused at this point, you're in good company. Time-traveling stories are always confusing.

Here's the thing to understand: Sam inevitably arrived at each new point in space-time woefully underequipped. He couldn't bring anything with him from leap to leap, and was forced to make the best out of whatever he could find around him. He also arrived entirely underinformed as to the nature of his mission. This was the source of much comedy and drama.

Well, Sam wasn't *entirely* alone. He was assisted by Al Calavicci, a flamboyantly dressed, cigar-chomping hologram who used a temperamental smartphone-like device to tap into a "parallel hybrid computer" called Ziggy. And yes, Sam had six PhDs, which is nothing to sneeze at. But Ziggy was buggy, Al disappeared at inconvenient times, and Sam's formidable intellect was artificially hampered by the impact of the Quantum Leap machine on his mind, resulting in what Al called Sam's "Swiss-cheese memory." So it would be more accurate to say he had *part of* six PhDs. Regardless of his limited and unreliable resources, he had to set something right before he could make his next leap, and it began with trying to figure out what exactly was wrong.

Here's why this matters: *Quantum Leap* is a perfect metaphor for technical program management challenges, and it sheds considerable light on how we should prepare for an uncertain future.

When envisioning a new technology, we inevitably find ourselves in new and unexpected situations—just like Sam. Also like Sam, we're armed with incomplete predictive models and a limited memory of what we've done in the past. Unlike Sam, we bring with us the hardware of previous excursions—a mixed blessing, to be sure.

This reminds me of David Whyte's observation that "it seems to be the nature of any new territory that we arrive on its borders flat broke." Old-world currency simply doesn't buy much in the new world.

This uncertainty meant that Sam could never plan ahead for the next mission. There was no way to tell from week to week whether he'd be a man, a woman, or a chimp. He might suddenly leap into someone who was driving a car, having a baby, or performing a dance routine in front of hundreds of people. The best he could do was play along until he figured out why he was there.

How did he manage to survive each episode? By fostering a flexible ability to respond to new, unexpected situations, never expecting this week's episode to have anything in common with last week's. And that's precisely what FIRE aims to do—increase our capacity for adaptability, focusing on flexible resources that don't get left behind each time we leap into a new episode.

In her book *Radical Careering*, Sally Hogshead talks about the importance of developing "portable equity." This basically means building a store of resources from today's situation that can be applied to tomorrow's. These need not be watered-down generalities—portable equity can be enormously specific technical skills and abilities. The key is *portability*—the ability to take it with you from mission to mission. Sally suggests spending more time developing portable equity and investing fewer resources into building equity that you will have to leave behind; whether you see it coming or not, chances are good you'll have to make a leap at some point.

FIRE aims to establish a similarly flexible ability to respond to the unexpected and places a similar premium on portable equity, both for the people involved and the technologies we build. On individual projects, FIRE points us toward establishing open standards and modular designs with well-defined interfaces. This helps the system adapt to emerging requirements, technologies, and threats.

In human terms, instead of fragile rules with narrow, specific applications, FIRE proposes antifragile rules of thumb that can be applied across a wider range of situations. This way, when we find ourselves in a new and unexpected situation, whispering the phrase "Oh, boy . . ." to ourselves and wondering when Al the Hologram is going to show up, we won't be completely unequipped.

The Millau Viaduct

Lest I give the impression that my taste in entertainment is limited to comic books and old science fiction or that FIRE is only relevant to small projects, our next example comes from an acclaimed foreign film that happened to point me in the direction of a successful megaproject from the south of France.

The movie was one of those films where the main character hardly says a word, communicating instead via significant glances, projecting emotion with every expression, every gesture. The lead actor was not only at the top of his profession but also happened to hold a master's degree in electrical engineering from the Queen's College, Oxford. As a fellow electrical engineer, I felt a certain kinship and was glad to see he'd overcome the professional limitations of his education to achieve international success in the arts.

As the hero's journey unfolded, a scene of such beauty emerged that I was compelled to pause the DVD and conduct a brief course of research into a breathtaking bridge the main character drove across.

Have you ever seen a movie where a bridge stole the scene simply by existing? This particular bridge's mere presence, understated and almost demure, was nevertheless like a thunderclap to my eyes—and my soul. I actually reversed the video and watched the scene three times before turning on my computer and asking Google for more information.

This is why we watch films from other lands, isn't it? To expand our exposure to a wider world, to plumb the depths of the human experience, to know we are alive and not alone, and to fully experience the bitterness and sweetness of existence.

Okay, the film was *Mr. Bean's Holiday* and I laughed my head off through most of it, but the part about rewatching and researching the bridge is totally true. Oddly enough, so is the part about Rowan Atkinson's engineering credentials.

Anyway, Google informed me the bridge is called the Millau (pronounced "meow") Viaduct. It spans 2.5 kilometers and passes 270 meters above the river Tarn in southern France. Its sheer beauty guaranteed it a spot in my heart, right alongside the scene where Mr. Bean eats an unshelled langoustine, one crunchy, uncomfortable, bug-eyed bite at a time. But what earned the bridge a spot in my mind—

and in this book—was the simple fact that it was completed within budget, one month ahead of schedule. I had to know more.

I was well aware that megaprojects like this tend to be late and over budget, an observation corroborated by a report from the Bartlett School of Planning at University College London (UCL). The report modestly observes, "It could be mentioned that in such a large scale project, increasing costs and delays over the construction phases are the norm." And yet no such delays or increases happened during the construction of this bridge. How could that be? What did they do differently?

Well, they didn't do it by taking the easy road, that's for sure. The UCL report points out that the Millau Viaduct was not what it referred to as one of those "economic but trivial structures, easy to build and without risks." In fact, it's the largest cable-stayed bridge in all of Europe. Yes, this was an ambitious project, in a demanding environment, and it aimed to address transportation needs as well as economic and touristic objectives, all in an environmentally responsible fashion.

Most projects fail or succeed at the beginning, so naturally the beginning is the first place I looked. It turns out that project leaders began by spending almost a decade studying the challenge, considering possible routes, establishing interdepartmental teams, calling for design proposals, and organizing a competition to select a winning design. I won't pretend that the process was fast, but I will point out they made steady progress from 1987 to 1996, when they selected a design. And I must firmly insist that thoughtful advance planning is fully compatible with FIRE.

Most of that time was spent studying the problem rather

than defining solutions, which may be a key to much of the teams' subsequent performance. There is something to be said for deeply understanding the need before pouring any concrete or bending any metal. On an architectural project like this one, the unique demands of the landscape limit our ability to copy previous structures. Although lessons from previous bridges can inform the design, we might say that this bridge was the first attempt to solve this particular challenge. And since a bridge is designed to last more than a hundred years, it probably makes sense to do a little extra homework up front. For that matter, we might even point out that the time spent in preparation was less than one-tenth of the bridge's expected lifespan. This might qualify as a "fast" time frame after all.

During the planning phase, project leaders determined that the conventional approach to bridge building would be too slow, expensive, and dangerous. They decided to develop a faster, cheaper, safer approach. And so they looked for ways to combine safety with speed, thrift, and simplicity rather than assuming that quality and safety automatically require increases to the cost, schedule, and complexity of the final product. This assumption is a significant departure from the norm and helps explain the outcome. Yes, all project managers talk about keeping an eye on cost and schedule, but most of the time they don't really mean it, as proved by the tendency to add time and money when faced with a challenge. The Millau Viaduct team said it and meant it.

The project leaders' decisions reveal a lot about their priorities. Sometimes complexity is held up as a sign of sophistication, in which case the project managers go out of their way to develop deeply complicated solutions. Similarly, managers who equate budget with prestige will have a high tolerance for budget increases. On this particular bridge, project leaders placed a premium on speed, thrift, simplicity, and restraint.

For example, two technical solutions were considered, a "low" solution and a "high" solution. Initially, the low solution was considered as the only possible route. Because of the time and money required to implement the low solution, project leaders refused to accept the inevitability of the obvious approach and explored additional alternatives. The high solution was eventually developed and selected because it was safer, shorter, cheaper, and more environmentally friendly. Had the project leaders settled for the obvious low solution, they would have spent more time and money on construction, caused more damage to the local environment, and operated a riskier project. Instead, they looked beyond the obvious and found something better.

The Millau Viaduct's platform is built of steel rather than the more typical concrete. Steel is lighter and stronger, and the team was able to preconstruct components in a factory, which meant the bridge could be completed in thirty-eight months instead of the fifty-two months required for on-site concrete work. That's real speed. And as the UCL report explains, "the decision to adopt the steel solution became a crucial factor in respect to avoiding construction delays." Time being money, this naturally helped constrain construction costs as well. And again, this application of creativity was driven by a genuine commitment to speed and thrift.

The project used "the minimal amount of material, which made it less costly to construct," a sure sign that designers were focused on an economical result. On the question of simplicity, they talked about what the "best solution and the most elegant" would be. This quintessentially French preference for elegance is a stark contrast to the tendency of some technologists to brag about how complex their designs are. By linking the concepts of *best* and *elegant*, project leaders oriented their team in the direction of mature simplicity rather than sloppy complexity.

But what about all that time spent planning? Is a decade of study really compatible with a fast project? It just might be. For starters, the extensive preconstruction work sped up the contract negotiations, which took less than a month. The UCL report called the negotiation phase "particularly quick." If you have ever been involved in a contract negotiation for a megaproject, you know this assessment is without a doubt the finest example of British understatement you'll find in all of literature. The report goes on to explain that such speed was made possible because the technical quality of the proposal was high and the risk approach "met the state's expectations," due largely to the extensive advance coordination and research (i.e., they started before they started). This is just one example of how advance planning leads to speedy results in the long run.

And then there is the question of innovation. In language reminiscent of the P-51 Mustang, which as you will recall "in no way exhibited any previously unknown engineering features," the UCL report states the viaduct "does not constitute a technical innovation in itself but is characterized by a genuine and innovative application of existing techniques."

Like the P-51 project's leaders, the Millau designers did not try to overinnovate, preferring instead to use proven methods where possible and new concepts only when necessary. The truly novel piece of the project is simply in the way they put together older methods.

Ultimately, the real secret sauce was in the project leaders' refusal to accept the status quo, a mind-set that is rarer than it need be. And that, my friends, is the point of the whole story.

If we learn nothing else from the Millau Viaduct, it is that broken schedules and busted budgets are not inevitable. It is possible to deliver even a €400 million, 2.5-kilometer bridge ahead of schedule and on budget. That is an important lesson. In fact, it just might be *the* lesson of this entire book.

It is possible to deliver a top-shelf product without exceeding the schedule and budget and without overcomplicating things. We can be fast, inexpensive, restrained, and elegant when we want to be. All too often, we fail to want to. All too often, our going-in position is that excessive expense, delay, and complexity are unavoidable on certain classes of projects. By expecting to overspend, we build in failure from the start. Projects like the Millau Viaduct help demonstrate that better outcomes are possible. I might even say projects like this *prove* we can be fast, inexpensive, restrained, and elegant, and that's not a word I throw around easily. Once we believe these alternatives exist, they are much easier to find and implement.

A beautiful bridge in the south of France shows that it is possible to deliver a best-in-class solution while simultaneously restraining the cost, schedule, and complexity of the object in question. These are not mutually incompatible goals. In fact, they seem to be mutually reinforcing. I contend that the viaduct is as good as it is—and looks the way it does—because it was built with a preference for speed, thrift, simplicity, and restraint.

A foundational principle is that projects—even big ones—don't need to cost so much, take so long, and be so complicated. Constraining these dimensions of the project is not only possible but also correlates with excellent outcomes. FIRE is designed to help us achieve faster, cheaper, simpler results, but we'll never use any of the principles or practices unless we first believe such results are possible. Stories like the Millau Viaduct help us believe.

Speed Does Not Come from Speed

The earlier comments about *Mr. Bean's Holiday* were somewhat tongue in cheek, but it is with the utmost sincerity that I say few books have touched my core as deeply as David Whyte's *Crossing the Unknown Sea*. A talented poet who consults with business leaders, Whyte has a gift for cutting through life's ephemera and bringing essential truths to light in deeply memorable ways. I've read his book several times and always come away moved, challenged, and enlightened. One passage in particular has haunted me ever since I first read it, in large part because it addresses a central topic of FIRE. He writes, "Speed by itself has never been associated with good work by those who have achieved mastery in any given field. Speed does not come from speed. Speed is a result, an outcome, an ecology of combining factors in a person's approach to work; deep attention, well-laid and well-sharpened tools, care, patience."

As a guy who is dedicated to rapid innovation, I find Whyte's observation about speed's relationship with good work challenging, even a little disturbing (in the best sense of the word), because I know he is correct, as good poets so often are.

Whyte reminds us that speed by itself is not intrinsically

virtuous. When we overvalue speed, when we rely on fast movement as the primary source of progress, we have almost certainly strayed from the path of mastery. Note that he is not saying speed is bad. After distancing "speed by itself" from mastery, he goes on to hold it up as an admirable outcome. It is speed's nature as a *component* of excellence, rather than an isolated objective, that is the key to understanding his point.

The observation that speed does not come from speed is dead-on. Speed actually comes from preparation. Speed comes from patience. Speed comes from a well-sharpened saw placed close at hand, a well-trained eye rich with years of observation and reflection. Speed is not hasty, frantic, or rushed. Paradoxically, speed takes time. It is the result of slow practice, of persistence and diligence.

Speed is indeed good and desirable, but like happiness it cannot be pursued for its own sake. To do so courts disaster.

Let's return again to Aesop's fable about the tortoise and the hare, that story we all heard as children. The secret is there. While the rabbit seemed faster, his was a careless speed, a superficial velocity unconnected with the race's true objective. The rabbit's sprinting was unsustainable and ultimately lazy. The tortoise, on the other hand, was patient and careful. He was disciplined and focused—even masterful. He got to the finish line first, demonstrating a poet's perspective on speed. The tortoise shows us that when you can see the fastest path to the finish line, you can also see that you don't have to run.

A similar dynamic occurs with the other three components of FIRE. Constraining costs is a good idea when done deliberately, reflectively, and strategically. However, thrift by itself is not associated with good work any more than speed is. When isolated from the larger cause, thrift devolves into stingy cheapness, producing products that break easily, do not achieve their objectives, or otherwise fail to provide the necessary quality. Simplicity and restraint go wrong in the same way when they move from a secondary, supporting role that helps us achieve a goal and instead assume a primary role, becoming goals unto themselves.

It is paradoxical, this idea that speed does not come from speed. One might even say it is poetic. Is speed a means to an end, or an end in itself? Both? Neither? Clearly, it is not *the* end, not the prime objective of our activity. We do not design products or lead projects in order to be fast. We do these things to produce something that satisfies a customer. However, the customer does not want to wait too long; the customer wants speed. So speed is part of what satisfies. And focusing on speed is part of how we provide that satisfaction. But focusing excessively on speed is precisely how Aesop's hare went wrong.

Similarly, minimizing expense, delay, and complexity are parts of our objective, but they are not, by themselves, the objective. A technical development project aims to deliver an affordable piece of technology that is available when needed and effective when used. Programmatic and technical constraints support that goal, bringing it within reach and ensuring alignment between the object and the user's needs. But the constraints themselves are not the goal. The constraints themselves should not be left to their own devices.

Let's put it this way: terrible things happen when we confuse goals and tools. Terrible, terrible, stupid, bureaucratic things. When a method is useful, we use it because it helps us do good work. In that sense, the method is important. But when it becomes more important than useful, when compliance is merely required rather than actively helpful, we find ourselves following the method even though it does not contribute to good work.

In a typical bureaucracy, this leads to an accumulation of overapplied policies, restrictions, and requirements, each of which was once useful in a particular situation, but many of which have become merely important. Bureaucracies love to mindlessly implement universal solutions to isolated problems. The rest of us end up applying these solutions because we are forced to, not because they support the project's deeper goals. Over time, the combined weight of it all makes forward progress exceedingly difficult and we find ourselves speeding—and napping—with Aesop's rabbit.

The same thing can happen with FIRE. If we allow the means to become the ends, if we pursue speed, thrift, simplicity, and restraint *by themselves*, without the care and patience and thoughtful reflection associated with genuine mastery, we will be sorely disappointed with the results. So will our customers.

When we overvalue speed and treat it as an end unto itself, the result is mere haste. Overemphasizing thrift leads to solutions that are merely cheap. When simplicity is a goal rather than a tool, we willingly settle for simplistic answers, embraced because they are not complex rather than because they are correct. And restraint as an objective results in too-small-itis, in which our documents, meetings, teams, and the like are genuinely insufficient. This helps no one.

A superficial pursuit of speed, thrift, simplicity, and restraint results in products that are simplistic, cheap, hasty, and too small. Of course, most bureaucracies tend to be miles away from this approach, preferring instead to be slow, expensive, complex, and ponderous and approaching every problem by adding time, money, and people. In these situations, the value of a new design is measured in terms of how many millions of lines of code it uses, how large the army of developers is, or how many grand technological promises it makes rather than on how well it is aligned with a customer's needs.

At first glance, it may seem the distance between the hasty and slow approaches is vast, but organizations actually transition easily from one to the other (and back again). This transition is common because both approaches are rooted in similarly superficial thinking. When a shallow attempt to fix problems (be they technical, organizational, or another type) by moving slowly and extending the schedule fails, the same shallowness easily concludes that the real answer must therefore be "less time." A more thoughtful perspective reveals that rushing is just as unfruitful as dawdling.

When Whyte observes that speed by itself is not associated with mastery, he is saying that speed by itself tends toward hastiness, toward inappropriately cutting corners, toward burning people out—ourselves and those around us—by insisting on turning the crank faster without regard for other aspects of the work. Speed by itself is blinding and can produce spectacular crashes. And so, when we grow impatient with slowness, the last thing we should do is insist on speed.

A skilled practitioner does not spend each day in a frenzied blur of activity, nimbly flying from one completed task to the next or endlessly transforming complicated rat's nests into simple works of art. Instead, he or she is much more likely to spend time quietly drinking tea and listening to people, reading books, getting some exercise, or going home at a reasonable time—maybe even a little bit earlier than everyone else. And doing so precisely because avoiding frantic haste—and the accompanying distractions, burnout, and exhaustion—is the secret to achieving effective, sustainable speed.

As for complexity, if we properly understand the simplicity cycle, we'll know that adding complexity is just as important as removing it. Yes, the mature simplicity on the other side of complexity is indeed the goal, but before we can come down from the mountain, we must first climb up it.

The wisdom of the poet reminds us that true speed comes from patience, from "well-laid and well-sharpened tools." And so, as we strive to deliver timely, affordable outcomes that fully satisfy our customers, we would do well to listen to the poet. We would do well to reflect on the relationship between speed and mastery. Speed, like thrift and simplicity, is indeed a good result, but it does not come from itself. So take the time to sharpen your tools. Take the time to cultivate patience and deep attention. Only then will you find that time is on your side.

Before becoming an electrical engineer and Air Force officer, I worked my way through high school and college as a juggler and magician. Making people smile on the birthday party circuit and at libraries, hospitals, and the occasional street corner was a lot of fun, and the money wasn't bad. There are definitely less enjoyable ways to make a living.

One of the first things any magician learns is that the secret behind each trick is almost always simple. Once it's revealed, the trick often feels obvious. Frankly, when audience members learn the secret, they can end up feeling a little bit stupid for not figuring it out right away. Some even feel disappointed or slightly betrayed that the performer had the audacity to fool them with such a simple move. Surely, they tell themselves, we deserve a more sophisticated deceit. That's one of the many reasons a good magician doesn't reveal the secret.

Now, with magic as with other things, there is a huge difference between simple and easy. Even a simple method can be fiendishly difficult to master, requiring countless hours of rehearsing in front of a mirror. In fact, the simplest tricks are often the hardest to do . . . and the most impressive. Laypeople are frequently unaware of this aspect of stage magic, so when a trick blows us away, there's a natural tendency to expect a complex, multistep explanation of how it's done.

Several years before my own modest career as an entertainer began, I was invited to a birthday party at which a magician performed. I don't recall whose party it was, but I'll never forget sitting on my friend's living room floor, watching the tall man in the dark tuxedo. As coins disappeared and reappeared across the room, I decided there had to be a complex set of invisible wires spiderwebbing the ceiling and walls. I suppose I thought the coins would just roll endwise along the appropriate wire before popping into his hand. Being seven years old, I didn't stop to wonder how he managed to set up all the wires in advance or how they managed to stay invisible or why we couldn't see the coins in transit. I just assumed there had to be some complex mechanism because the simpler solution escaped me. Eventually, the wisdom of age and firsthand experience as a coin handler showed me that no such construct was necessary. The true method was, as they say, all in the wrist. Or maybe he used mirrors. It was a long time ago, so I can't say for sure.

Anyway, the FIRE approach brings to mind my days as a young magician, not because there is any subterfuge involved but because the "secret" of how it's done is almost disturbingly simple. As with good sleight of hand, FIRE is not easy to master. It takes a fair amount of effort to hone the expertise and skills necessary to do it well. But those looking for complex mechanics beneath the surface are inevitably disappointed. There is no network of invisible threads. The fundamental mechanisms involved are not complicated. It really comes down to placing a premium on speed, thrift, simplicity, and restraint, and then using those principles to shape our approach to problem solving and decision making. The big secret is that the best products aren't the most expensive and complicated, and we really are better off with less expensive, less complex solutions. I understand if the simplicity of that explanation is a little disappointing. Believe me, I feel it too.

People often ask if there is a comprehensive, formal process diagram that explains how to do this thing called FIRE, or what sort of new laws and policies would need to be written in order for government agencies to implement it. Most of the time, it is because these people are process or policy makers seeking to translate FIRE into their native language. For the same reason, other people come looking for an extensive checklist that doesn't exist—much to their frustration.

You see, FIRE is really about aligning our decision making around a small set of values, preferences, and priorities. It's about pursuing speed, thrift, simplicity, and restraint. It's about a problem-solving pattern that tends to deliver outstanding results. It's not about a complicated, effort-intensive conglomeration of policy changes, regulatory documents, and process diagrams . . . especially not the process diagrams. We could make a big set of diagrams and checklists if we really wanted to. They just wouldn't help all that much.

Giving that explanation feels a bit like a magician revealing a simple secret: "Ah, there were *two* coins!" or, "Oh, you have a hidden pocket!" I can't help but share a little of the disappointment felt by those who assume a miracle has to have a complicated explanation. If it's really that simple, why didn't we notice it before? The answer might be that we failed to see the simplicity because we were looking for complexity. We didn't see the flick of the magician's wrist because we were too busy looking for a nonexistent network of invisible wires.

Here's the twist: there is one scenario in which revealing the simplicity of a secret leads to excitement rather than disappointment, where the hearer feels pleased and clever rather than frustrated and stupid. This happy outcome occurs when a magician teaches a sleight to a fellow magician.

The purpose behind the reveal makes all the difference. A spectator learns the secret for no reason other than to satisfy his curiosity, and the more complex secrets are generally more satisfying. In contrast, a performer learns the secret in order to add it to her repertoire, and simplicity indicates a truly elegant illusion. For a spectator, a secret is merely information with no further purpose. For a practitioner, it is a key to mastery and growth.

In the latter situation, simplicity is gratifying and feels right. The conjuror who learns a new, efficient sleight from a peer knows it has been honed down to remove any unnecessary effort. Simplicity is therefore a desirable sign of sophistication rather than a disappointment. If the method is excessively complicated, an experienced performer will look for ways to reduce it to its essential core.

To be sure, a sophomoric apprentice may respond to simplicity by throwing in extraneous flourishes, adding complexity and effort without enhancing the audience's experience. The wise master will help such an apprentice discover whether that approach truly advances the art.

In similar fashion, FIRE's simplicity is deliberate and the purpose of this book's reveal is to equip people for action. Don't be fooled; mastering these simple moves requires effort, practice, and dedication. But it is their very simplicity that makes them so effective. Replace the simplicity with complexity, and we lose much of the magic.

Final Thoughts

For several decades now, the most successful and important military and space technology projects were developed according to the high-speed, low-drag pattern. To be sure, exceptions to that pattern exist, but for the most part FIRE describes how the US military and NASA do things when they are at their best.

Fortunately, you don't have to be in the defense or space businesses to use this approach, which has also been successfully applied to bridges, consumer electronics, and even kitchen appliances. You don't have to be Superman or Alexander the Great or Captain Picard. You don't even have to be Chris Quaid, although that would certainly help. Whoever you are, so long as you're making decisions and solving problems, the FIRE principles can help point you in the direction of higher quality and faster, simpler, less expensive outcomes.

As the stories in this book show, top-shelf technology development projects do not have to cost so much, take so long, or be so complicated. By placing a premium on speed, thrift, simplicity, and restraint, we can deliver first-in-class and best-in-class products without spending decades and billions. This level of performance may not be easy, but it is certainly possible. If you remember nothing else from this book, remember that.

Also, remember the goofy dishwasher story.

FIRE takes aim at some fundamental assumptions about which attributes are desirable and valuable in a technology project. When we view complexity as a sign of sophistication, we build needlessly complicated things, which cost more, take longer, and do less than they might otherwise. When we assume that creation requires addition, we miss the opportunity to carve away unnecessary elements and reveal a hidden masterpiece. In contrast, when we embrace speed, thrift, simplicity, and restraint, we might find ourselves producing things we never thought possible. Things like a one-page cartoon on how to build a toy hovercraft. Or a fighter jet that "in no way exhibits any previously unknown engineering principles," but goes on to serve as a front-line fighter for decades.

Along with challenging our assumptions about the inevitability of schedule delays and budget overruns, FIRE provides concrete practices and tools. The simplicity cycle diagram, the trimming flow chart, stormdraining, and reductive thinking are all intended to populate your toolbox and equip you for action. Whether you're writing code, designing a spacecraft, manufacturing a dishwasher, or putting together a set of PowerPoint charts, these tools can help increase quality while minimizing delay, expense, and complexity.

At its core, FIRE is about restraint. When in the name of restraint we build only the essential functions and include only the necessary interface components, we discover deep simplicity. Not simplicity for its own sake, but a simplicity that fosters quality, reliability, and usability. Similarly, when our commitment to restraint leads us to perform only the necessary activities, to only write useful documents and only hold meaningful meetings, we find that the pace of progress accelerates far beyond our hopes. Like simplicity, speed is a product of restraint. So is thrift—doing less has a strong correlation with spending less in the long run.

The things we choose to not do, the things we say no to, and the elements we omit in the name of restraint—these are what enable us to be fast, inexpensive, and elegant. They also ensure that the final product is a first-class one. Except for when they don't. FIRE doesn't always work for everyone in every circumstance. Sometimes, we can apply it perfectly and still fail, as the F-20 Tigershark did. Failure is even more certain if we apply the practices like a bumper sticker à la the DIVAD. But if we do things right, we'll find that even our failures are mitigated and constrained, and they lay the foundation for future successes.

Designing and delivering new technology projects is hard work. FIRE does not make it magically easy. But doing things the other way—by throwing lots of time and money and people at the problem—is not easy either, nor does that approach guarantee a positive outcome. In fact, a lack of restraint tends to result in projects that not only cost more and take longer but also underperform.

The good news is that we have an alternative. It genuinely is possible to be fast, inexpensive, restrained, and elegant. When we put those pieces together, we just might discover we are capable of producing something amazing.

A Deliberately Incomplete List of Heuristics

- You cannot design anything without revealing your values.
- Constraints foster creativity.
- Focus fosters speed.
- Speed validates the need.
- To finish early, start early.
- Delays cause delays.
- A project leader's influence is inversely proportional to the budget.
- Complexity is not a sign of sophistication.
- A kick-ass half is better than a half-assed whole.
- The best way to unleash talent is not to have too much of it.
- Minimize the distance between decision and action.
- The tactical ability to rapidly deliver new capabilities is itself a strategic capability.
- The future will be surprising. Prepare accordingly.
- You can't change just one thing.
- No more than one miracle per project.
- Someone already solved your problem.

ACKNOWLEDGMENTS

In 2003, as a young Air Force captain assigned to a military intelligence agency, I sat at my desk thinking deep thoughts about my chosen profession as a military technologist. Specifically, I pondered the eternal question of why so many projects are so far behind schedule and over budget, while others manage to deliver early and have money left over. I had no particular answer in mind about what caused these different outcomes, but I knew it was an important question.

My initial research led to a surprising discovery—military technology projects deliver on time when project leaders *want* them to deliver on time. The same goes for sticking to a budget—we can do it when we make thrift a priority. It really comes down to a question of will, priorities, and values. My research went on to indicate that overextended projects typically do not even attempt to restrain their spending or their schedules and tend to treat complexity as both inevitable and desirable. I was a little shocked to discover that the desire to be fast, inexpensive, and simple is not universal, but there you go.

Expanding my investigation beyond the realm of defense, I discovered that NASA's Faster, Better, Cheaper missions fit the pattern too. I found a similarly fast and inexpensive dynamic in the commercial world, thanks to writers like Tom Peters, companies like Apple, and movements like Agile software development.

In the years that followed, many people came alongside and helped develop the idea further. My name may be on the cover, but this book literally (and I do mean *literally*) would not exist if not for the following people, presented in roughly chronological order of their contribution. Therefore it is with great pleasure that I write the two most important words in this whole book: Thank You.

MY PARENTS. You guys are the best—thanks for always being such great supporters and cheerleaders. Your example is an inspiration and your love is unwavering.

LIEUTENANT COLONEL JOE WOTTON, best boss ever and friend for life. Your enthusiastic support for my (mercifully unpublished) first attempt at writing a book showed me what caring leadership looks like and taught me more than you know.

COLONEL TED COPE. Who knew a self-described "liberal Buddhist hippie" could wear a colonel's eagles on his shoulders with such style and grace? Your tenacity, imagination, and enthusiasm are a perpetual source of inspiration.

LIEUTENANT COLONEL CHRIS QUAID, my brother-in-arms. You showed up at just the right moment (how do you always do that?) and were a brilliant partner during one of the most exciting assignments of my career. You helped me break through my own limitations and made me a better writer, thinker, and officer.

JUDITH GREIG. You gave me a platform at *Defense AT&L* magazine, helped me develop an audience, helped me find my voice and, most important, went to bat for me when my proposals met with resistance. Your gutsy support let me publish some seriously weird stuff in an official government publication.

CAROL SHEINA. Your creativity and vision transformed *Defense AT&L* magazine, while your gentle excellence helped push my writing to the next level—on countless magazine articles as well as this book.

GABE MOUNCE. One word: awesome. Thanks for being such a high-energy writing partner, collaborator, and friend.

LIEUTENANT COLONEL STEVE BEHM. Our training runs whipped my body into shape for the Air Force marathon, but the conversations on those runs helped shape my understanding of this FIST thing as I wrote my thesis.

MAJOR PETE MASTRO. If not for your tenacity and generosity, I would not have been able to write my thesis about FIST in the first place. Without that thesis, I'm pretty sure this book would not exist.

DR. DEJI BADIRU. While some in the academic community looked askance at my ideas, wanting them to be more formal, quantifiable, and theoretical, you saw value in a story-based, practitioner-oriented, real-world approach. Thank you for your unflagging support.

KATE MESSNER. Your encouragement, excitement, insight, and advice were such gifts as I began navigating this new world of writing books.

ANDY NULMAN. When I thought I might publish a

particular book, you sagely suggested I write this one instead. Surprise! I'd like to think I'd have figured that out eventually, but I probably wouldn't have.

DON NORMAN. Your books changed the way I look at design, while your kind willingness to introduce me to your agent changed my publishing fortunes and my life.

My agent, SANDY DIJKSTRA. What an amazing experience it is to be partnered with you and the rest of the Dijkstra Agency team. You saw much farther than I did and brought my modest little proposal to life in a bigger way than I ever dreamed. Big thanks to ELISE CAPRON in particular for fielding my newbie questions and cheering me on at every step.

My publisher, HOLLIS HEIMBOUCH. Your gentle insight and enthusiastic encouragement helped me make the leap from magazine writer to book author. You unfailingly pointed the way to better and made this whole experience a tremendous pleasure.

ALLEN WOODS and KEN ATKINS. Thank you for generously sharing your stories with me and for allowing me to tell those stories in this little book.

And finally, I owe the biggest thanks to my amazing wife, KIM. Your love, patience, love, wisdom, love, support, and love mean everything to me, not just as I worked on this book but also as we work on this life together. Plus, you're the best kind of smart—gentle, insightful, and funny—and every day I am so completely awestruck and thankful you took a chance on me all those years ago. I love you a million, for always!

SELECTED SOURCES

Campbell, Clark. *The One-Page Project Manager*. New York: Wiley, 2006.

Chanute, Octave. *Progress in Flying Machines*. Long Beach, CA: Lorenz and Herweg, 1976.

Christensen, Clayton. *The Innovator's Dilemma: The Revolutionary Book That Will Change the Way You Do Business*. New York: HarperBusiness, 2011.

Danzig, Richard. *Driving in the Dark: Ten Propositions about Prediction and National Security*. Washington, DC: Center for New American Security, 2011.

Drucker, Peter F. *The Practice of Management*. New York: HarperBusiness, 1993.

Fried, Jason, and David Hansson. *Rework*. New York: Crown Business, 2010.

Gawande, Atul. *Better: A Surgeon's Notes on Performance*. New York: Picador, 2008.

Hogshead, Sally. *Radical Careering: 100 Truths to*

Jumpstart Your Job, Your Career, and Your Life. New York: Gotham, 2005.

McCurdy, Howard. *Faster, Better, Cheaper: Low-Cost Innovation in the US Space Program.* Baltimore: Johns Hopkins University Press, 2003.

Reynolds, Garr. *Presentation Zen: Simple Ideas on Presentation Design and Delivery.* New York: New Rider, 2008.

Senge, Peter. *The Fifth Discipline: The Art and Practice of the Learning Organization.* New York: Doubleday, 2006.

Taleb, Nassim. *The Black Swan: The Impact of the Highly Improbable.* New York: Random House, 2007.

——— . *Antifragile: Things That Gain from Disorder.* New York: Random House, 2012.

Whyte, David. *Crossing the Unknown Sea: Work as a Pilgrimage of Identity.* New York: Riverhead, 2001.

DAN WARD is a lieutenant colonel in the US Air Force with nearly two decades of experience in researching, developing, designing, testing, and fielding military equipment. He holds three engineering degrees and specializes in rapid, low-cost innovation. His previous assignments include the Air Force Research Lab, the National Geospatial Intelligence Agency, the Air Force Institute of Technology, the Pentagon, and International Security Assistance Force Headquarters in Kabul, Afghanistan. Dan wears the Master Acquisition Badge and the Command Space Badge. In 2012, he received the Bronze Star Medal for his service in Afghanistan.

He lives in Massachusetts with his wife and two daughters.